W9-CSP-008

Eating Disorders

Recent Titles in
Q&A Health Guides

EATING DISORDERS

Your Questions Answered

Justine J. Reel

Q&A Health Guides

GREENWOOD™

An Imprint of ABC-CLIO, LLC
Santa Barbara, California • Denver, Colorado

Library of Congress Cataloging-in-Publication Data

Names: Reel, Justine J., author.
Title: Eating disorders : your questions answered / Justine J. Reel.
Description: Santa Barbara, California : Greenwood, an imprint of
    ABC-CLIO, LLC, [2018] | Series: Q&A health guides | Includes
    bibliographical references and index.
Identifiers: LCCN 2018020375 (print) | LCCN 2018022081 (ebook) |
    ISBN 9781440853050 (ebook) | ISBN 9781440853043 (alk. paper)
Subjects: LCSH: Eating disorders—Miscellanea.
Classification: LCC RC552.E18 (ebook) | LCC RC552.E18 R432 2018 (print) |
    DDC 616.85/26—dc23
LC record available at https://lccn.loc.gov/2018020375

ISBN: 978-1-4408-5304-3 (print)
        978-1-4408-5305-0 (ebook)

22 21 20 19 18   1 2 3 4 5

This book is also available as an eBook.

Greenwood
An Imprint of ABC-CLIO, LLC

ABC-CLIO, LLC
130 Cremona Drive, P.O. Box 1911
Santa Barbara, California 93116-1911
www.abc-clio.com

This book is printed on acid-free paper ∞

Manufactured in the United States of America

This book discusses treatments (including types of medication and mental health therapies), diagnostic tests for various symptoms and mental health disorders, and organizations. The author has made every effort to present accurate and up-to-date information. However, the information in this book is not intended to recommend or endorse particular treatments or organizations, or substitute for the care or medical advice of a qualified health professional, or used to alter any medical therapy without a medical doctor's advice. Specific situations may require specific therapeutic approaches not included in this book. For those reasons, we recommend that readers follow the advice of qualified healthcare professionals directly involved in their care. Readers who suspect they may have specific medical problems should consult a physician about any suggestions made in this book.

This book is dedicated to all eating disorder "survivors" and individuals who continue to suffer from disordered eating and/or negative body image. It is my hope that with greater awareness we can conquer and prevent this harmful disease.

Contents

Series Foreword

All of us have questions about our health. Is this normal? Should I be doing something differently? Who should I talk to about my concerns? And our modern world is full of answers. Thanks to the Internet, there's a wealth of information at our fingertips, from forums where people can share their personal experiences to Wikipedia articles to the full text of medical studies. But finding the right information can be an intimidating and difficult task—some sources are written at too high a level, others have been oversimplified, while still others are heavily biased or simply inaccurate.

Q&A Health Guides address the needs of readers who want accurate, concise answers to their health questions, authored by reputable and objective experts and written in clear and easy-to-understand language. This series focuses on the topics that matter most to young adult readers, including various aspects of physical and emotional well-being, as well as other components of a healthy lifestyle. These guides will also serve as a valuable tool for parents, school counselors, and others who may need to answer teens' health questions.

All books in the series follow the same format to make finding information quick and easy. Each volume begins with an essay on health literacy and why it is so important when it comes to gathering and evaluating health information. Next, the top five myths and misconceptions that surround the topic are dispelled. The heart of each guide is a collection of questions and answers, organized thematically. A selection of five case studies provide real-world examples to illuminate key concepts. Rounding out each volume are a directory of resources, glossary, and index.

It is our hope that the books in this series will not only provide valuable information but will also help guide readers toward a lifetime of healthy decision-making.

Acknowledgments

I would like to acknowledge the genuine support of my acquisitions editor, Maxine Taylor, my colleagues from around the world, and my friends and family. To my husband, Robert, thank you for your unwavering love and devotion. You are my rock.

Introduction

Eating is a normal part of the human experience, and food has played an important role in our society throughout history. Although eating represents a basic need for survival and serves as fuel for the body's systems, the meaning of food is much more complicated than a biological necessity. Eating can represent a popular and beloved pastime for individuals and families, but negative and unhealthy aspects of our relationship with food may also be present. To this end, eating behavior exists on a spectrum ranging from healthy to unhealthy. Both severe undereating or anorexia nervosa and overeating are represented with the disordered eating continuum.

The types of eating disorders recognized by the healthcare field and included in the current edition of the *Diagnostic Statistical Manual of Mental Disorders* are anorexia nervosa, bulimia nervosa, binge eating disorder, and feeding disorders such as avoidant-restrictive food intake disorder (ARFID). ARFID is represented by symptoms such as food avoidance, decreased appetite, and fear of vomiting or choking without the associated body image concerns. Causes of eating disorders are multifaceted and include genetics, psychological, and sociocultural factors. Body dissatisfaction and the perpetuation of the thinness ideal are strong predictors of disordered eating behavior.

Although eating disorders were not studied extensively until the 1980s and few treatment options existed before that decade, there was evidence of disordered eating an entire century prior. Specifically, anorexia nervosa was observed in the 1870s by two physicians who noted that their patients were avoiding food and appeared to have a loss of appetite. Currently, it is estimated that more than 10 million boys and men will develop eating disorders at some point in their lifetime. Males represent 10 to 25 percent of eating disorders, but these conditions often go undetected. By contrast, more than 20 million girls and women will suffer from eating disorders. Eating disorders are particularly common in the adolescent population, with anorexia nervosa representing the third most common chronic disease behind asthma and type 1 diabetes. It is estimated that a half million of teenagers exhibit disordered eating or meet the criteria for a full-blown eating disorder. This is problematic as eating disorders result in severe health consequences and are potentially life-threatening. Therefore, early detection and treatment are important for addressing eating disorders. This book attempts to answer common questions related to eating disorders across a variety of areas—identification, contribution, effects, and treatment.

Guide to Health Literacy

On her 13th birthday, Samantha was diagnosed with type 2 diabetes. She consulted her mom and her aunt, both of whom also have type 2 diabetes, and decided to go with their strategy of managing diabetes by taking insulin. As a result of participating in an after-school program at her middle school that focused on health literacy, she learned that she can help manage the level of glucose in her bloodstream by counting her carbohydrate intake, following a diabetic diet, and exercising regularly. But, what exactly should she do? How does she keep track of her carbohydrate intake? What is a diabetic diet? How long should she exercise, and what type of exercise should she do? Samantha is a visual learner, so she turned to her favorite source of media, YouTube, to answer these questions. She found videos from individuals around the world sharing their experiences and tips, doctors (or at least people who have "Dr." in their YouTube channel names), government agencies such as the National Institutes of Health, and even video clips from cat lovers who have cats with diabetes. With guidance from the librarian and the health and science teachers at her school, she assessed the credibility of the information in these videos and even compared their suggestions to some of the print resources that she was able to find at her school library. Now, she knows exactly how to count her carbohydrate level, how to prepare and follow a diabetic diet, and how much (and what) exercise is needed daily. She intends to share her findings with her mom and her aunt, and now she wants to create a chart that summarizes what she has learned that she can share with her doctor.

Samantha's experience is not unique. She represents a shift in our society; an individual no longer views himself or herself as a passive recipient of medical care but as an active mediator of his or her own health. However, in this era when any individual can post his or her opinions and experiences with a particular health condition online with just a few clicks or publish a memoir, it is vital that people know how to assess the credibility of health information. Gone are the days when "publishing" health information required intense vetting. The health information landscape is highly saturated, and people have innumerable sources where they can find information about practically any health topic. The sources (whether print, online, or a person) that an individual consults for health information are crucial because the accuracy and trustworthiness of the information can potentially affect his or her overall health. The ability to find, select, assess, and use health information constitutes a type of literacy—health literacy—that everyone must possess.

THE DEFINITION AND PHASES OF HEALTH LITERACY

One of the most popular definitions for health literacy comes from Ratzan and Parker (2000), who describe health literacy as "the degree to which individuals have the capacity to obtain, process, and understand basic health information and services needed to make appropriate health decisions." Recent research has extrapolated health literacy into health literacy bits, further shedding light on the multiple phases and literacy practices that are embedded within the multifaceted concept of health literacy. Although this research has focused primarily on online health information seeking, these health literacy bits are needed to successfully navigate both print and online sources. There are six phases of health information seeking: (1) Information Need Identification and Question Formulation, (2) Information Search, (3) Information Comprehension, (4) Information Assessment, (5) Information Management, and (6) Information Use.

The first phase is the *information need identification and question formulation phase*. In this phase, one needs to be able to develop and refine a range of questions to frame one's search and understand relevant health terms. In the second phase, *information search*, one has to possess appropriate searching skills, such as using proper keywords and correct spelling in search terms, especially when using search engines and databases.

It is also crucial to understand how search engines work (i.e., how search results are derived, what the order of the search results means, how to use the snippets that are provided in the search results list to select websites, and how to determine which listings are ads on a search engine results page). One also has to limit reliance on surface characteristics, such as the design of a website or a book (a website or book that appears to have a lot of information or looks aesthetically pleasant does not necessarily mean it has good information) and language used (a website or book that utilizes jargon, the keywords that one used to conduct the search, or the word "information" does not necessarily indicate it will have good information). The next phase is *information comprehension*, whereby one needs to have the ability to read, comprehend, and recall the information (including textual, numerical, and visual content) one has located from the books and/or online resources.

To assess the credibility of health information (*information assessment phase*), one needs to be able to evaluate information for accuracy, evaluate how current the information is (e.g., when a website was last updated or when a book was published), and evaluate the creators of the source—for example, examine site sponsors or type of sites (.com, .gov, .edu, or .org) or the author of a book (practicing doctor, a celebrity doctor, a patient of a specific disease, etc.) to determine the believability of the person/ organization providing the information. Such credibility perceptions tend to become generalized, so they must be frequently reexamined (e.g., the belief that a specific news agency always has credible health information needs continuous vetting). One also needs to evaluate the credibility of the medium (e.g., television, Internet, radio, social media, and book) and evaluate—not just accept without questioning—others' claims regarding the validity of a site, book, or other specific source of information. At this stage, one has to "make sense of information gathered from diverse sources by identifying misconceptions, main and supporting ideas, conflicting information, point of view, and biases" (American Association of School Librarians [AASL], 2009, p. 13) and conclude which sources/ information are valid and accurate by using conscious strategies rather than simply using intuitive judgments or "rules of thumb." This phase is the most challenging segment of health information seeking and serves as a determinant of success (or lack thereof) in the information-seeking process. The following section on Sources of Health Information further explains this phase.

The fifth phase is *information management*, whereby one has to organize information that has been gathered in some manner to ensure easy retrieval and use in the future. The last phase is *information use*, in which one will synthesize information found across various resources, draw conclusions, and locate the answer to his or her original question and/or the content that fulfills the information need. This phase also often involves implementation, such as using the information to solve a health problem; make health-related decisions; identify and engage in behaviors that will help a person to avoid health risks; share the health information found with family members and friends who may benefit from it; and advocate more broadly for personal, family, or community health.

THE IMPORTANCE OF HEALTH LITERACY

The conception of health has moved from a passive view (someone is either well or ill) to one that is more active and process based (someone is working toward preventing or managing disease). Hence, the dominant focus has shifted from doctors and treatments to patients and prevention, resulting in the need to strengthen our ability and confidence (as patients and consumers of health care) to look for, assess, understand, manage, share, adapt, and use health-related information. An individual's health literacy level has been found to predict his or her health status better than age, race, educational attainment, employment status, and income level (National Network of Libraries of Medicine [NNLM], 2013). Greater health literacy also enables individuals to better communicate with healthcare providers such as doctors, nutritionists, and therapists, as they can pose more relevant, informed, and useful questions to healthcare providers. Another added advantage of greater health literacy is better information-seeking skills, not only for health but also in other domains, such as completing assignments for school.

SOURCES OF HEALTH INFORMATION: THE GOOD, THE BAD, AND THE IN-BETWEEN

For generations, doctors, nurses, nutritionists, health coaches, and other health professionals have been the trusted sources of health information. Additionally, researchers have found that young adults, when they have health-related questions, typically turn to a family member who has had firsthand experience with a health condition because of their family member's close proximity and because of their past experience with, and trust in, this individual. Expertise should be a core consideration when consulting a person, website, or book for health information. The credentials and background of the person or author and conflicting interests of the author (and his or her organization) must be checked and validated to ensure the likely credibility of the health information they are conveying. While books often have implied credibility because of the peer-review process involved, self-publishing has challenged this credibility, so qualifications of book authors should also be verified. When it comes to health information, currency of the source must also be examined. When examining health information/studies presented, pay attention to the exhaustiveness of research methods utilized to offer recommendations or conclusions. Small and nondiverse sample size is often—but not always—an indication of reduced credibility. Studies that confuse correlation with causation is another potential issue to watch for. Information seekers must also pay attention to the sponsors of the research studies. For example, if a study is sponsored by manufacturers of drug Y and the study recommends that drug Y is the best treatment to manage or cure a disease, this may indicate a lack of objectivity on the part of the researchers.

The Internet is rapidly becoming one of the main sources of health information. Online forums, news agencies, personal blogs, social media sites, pharmacy sites, and celebrity "doctors" are all offering medical and health information targeted to various types of people in regard to all types of diseases and symptoms. There are professional journalists, citizen journalists, hoaxers, and people paid to write fake health news on various sites that may appear to have a legitimate domain name and may even have authors who claim to have professional credentials, such as an MD. All these sites *may* offer useful information or information that appears to be useful and relevant; however, much of the information may be debatable and may fall into gray areas that require readers to discern credibility, reliability, and biases.

While broad recognition and acceptance of certain media, institutions, and people often serve as the most popular determining factors to assess credibility of health information among young people, keep in mind that there are legitimate Internet sites, databases, and books that publish health information and serve as sources of health information for doctors, other health sites, and members of the public. For example, MedlinePlus (https://medlineplus.gov) has trusted sources on over 975 diseases and conditions and presents the information in easy-to-understand language.

The chart here presents factors to consider when assessing credibility of health information. However, keep in mind that these factors function only as a guide and require continuous updating to keep abreast with the changes in the landscape of health information, information sources, and technologies.

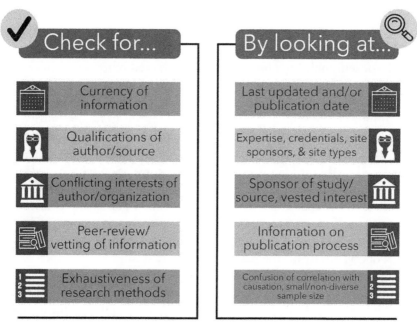

All images from www.flaticon.com

The chart can serve as a guide; however, approaching a librarian about how one can go about assessing the credibility of both print and online health information is far more effective than using generic checklist-type tools. While librarians are not health experts, they can apply and teach patrons strategies to determine the credibility of health information.

With the prevalence of fake sites and fake resources that appear to be legitimate, it is important to use the following health information assessment tips to verify health information that one has obtained (St. Jean et al., 2015, p. 151):

- **Don't assume you are right**: Even when you feel very sure about an answer, keep in mind that the answer may not be correct, and it is important to conduct (further) searches to validate the information.
- **Don't assume you are wrong**: You may actually have correct information, even if the information you encounter does not match—that is, you may be right and the resources that you have found may contain false information.
- **Take an open approach**: Maintain a critical stance by not including your preexisting beliefs as keywords (or letting them influence your choice of keywords) in a search, as this may influence what it is possible to find out.

- **Verify, verify, and verify**: Information found, especially on the Internet, needs to be validated, no matter how the information appears on the site (i.e., regardless of the appearance of the site or the quantity of information that is included).

Health literacy comes with experience navigating health information. Professional sources of health information, such as doctors, healthcare providers, and health databases, are still the best, but one also has the power to search for health information and then verify it by consulting with these trusted sources and by using the health information assessment tips and guide shared previously.

Mega Subramaniam, PhD
Associate Professor, College of Information
Studies, University of Maryland

REFERENCES AND FURTHER READING

American Association of School Librarians (AASL). (2009). *Standards for the 21st-century learner in action.* Chicago, IL: American Association of School Librarians.

Hilligoss, B., & Rieh, S.-Y. (2008). Developing a unifying framework of credibility assessment: Construct, heuristics, and interaction in context. *Information Processing & Management, 44*(4), 1467–1484.

Kuhlthau, C. C. (1988). Developing a model of the library search process: Cognitive and affective aspects. *Reference Quarterly, 28*(2), 232–242.

National Network of Libraries of Medicine (NNLM). (2013). "Health literacy." Bethesda, MD: National Network of Libraries of Medicine. Retrieved from nnlm.gov/outreach/consumer/hlthlit.html

Ratzan, S. C., & Parker, R. M. (2000). "Introduction." In C. R. Selden, M. Zorn, S. C. Ratzan, & R. M. Parker (Eds.), *National Library of Medicine current bibliographies in medicine: Health literacy.* NLM Pub. No. CBM 2000–1. Bethesda, MD: National Institutes of Health, U.S. Department of Health and Human Services.

St. Jean, B., Subramaniam, M., Taylor, N. G., Follman, R., Kodama, C., & Casciotti, D. (2015). The influence of positive hypothesis testing on youths' online health-related information seeking. *New Library World, 116*(3/4), 136–154.

St. Jean, B., Taylor, N. G., Kodama, C., & Subramaniam, M. (February 2017). Assessing the health information source perceptions of tweens using card-sorting exercises. *Journal of Information Science*. Retrieved from http://journals.sagepub.com/doi/abs/10.1177/0165551516687728

Subramaniam, M., St. Jean, B., Taylor, N. G., Kodama, C., Follman, R., & Casciotti, D. (2015). Bit by bit: Using design-based research to improve the health literacy of adolescents. *JMIR Research Protocols, 4*(2), paper e62. Retrieved from http://www.ncbi.nlm.nih.gov/pmc/articles/PMC4464334/

Valenza, J. (2016, November 26). "Truth, truthiness, and triangulation: A news literacy toolkit for a 'post-truth' world [Web log]." Retrieved from http://blogs.slj.com/neverendingsearch/2016/11/26/truth-truthiness-triangulation-and-the-librarian-way-a-news-literacy-toolkit-for-a-post-truth-world/

❖❖

Common Misconceptions about
Eating Disorders

1. "JUST EAT": IF SOMEONE WITH AN EATING DISORDER JUST EATS, IT WILL BE ALL BETTER

A common misconception of eating disorders is that a person with an eating disorder is a positive, super-disciplined individual who carefully watches consumption, rather than someone with a medical condition that can result in adverse health consequences. People will often joke, "I have an eating disorder. I can't stop eating," or "I wish I had an eating disorder, but I like food too much." These comments underscore a frequently held misunderstanding of the underlying psychological characteristics that can contribute to the development of disordered behavior. It is important to educate the public that people with eating disorders still *like* food. In fact, they often report feeling controlled by food and lacking the ability to stop thinking about food. People with eating disorders experience hunger as well; however, their refusal to eat (in the case of anorexia nervosa) is tied to a denial of hunger. This myth contributes to an oversimplified belief that someone with a problem will overcome an eating disorder if he or she just starts to eat again. In reality, eating disorders are more complex than an individual's relationship with food. Like depression and anxiety, eating disorders are included as a mental disorder in the *Diagnostic Statistical Manual of Mental Disorders,*

5th Edition. Eating disorders are marked by intense body dissatisfaction and poor self-esteem. Restricting food and other behaviors related to eating disorders, such as binge eating and purging, are symptoms of emotional distress. Instead of using words or expressing these negative emotions, controlling food intake and diet becomes an unhealthy coping strategy. Without getting to the root of the problem, an eating disorder will persist and likely get worse. Treating eating disorders takes time, and recovery does not happen overnight. To learn more about the way eating disorders are treated, please check out question #30.

2. EATING DISORDERS ARE SIMPLY USED AS A WAY TO GET ATTENTION

Another misperception is that people stop eating or change eating patterns as a way to get attention from family and friends. This mistaken belief that individuals who have an eating disorder use it to be noticed is damaging, because like the first myth (i.e., eating disorders are all about food), it ignores the complexity of this mental health disorder. Using an eating disorder to demand attention would be the rare exception, rather than the rule, when it comes to eating disorders. In reality, the causes of eating disorders are multifaceted and complex. There tends to be a genetic predisposition that leads to a vulnerability, as well as psychological and sociocultural characteristics and factors, which contribute to the development of disordered eating. Eating disorders may run in families, but they are also caused by observing parents who actively engage in eating disordered behavior. Psychological characteristics, such as high sensitivity, poor self-esteem, and perfectionism represent significant risks for developing an eating disorder. Being in a social context that values appearance and encourages changes in body weight, shape, and size can also contribute to eating disorders. Participating in certain activities, such as sports or dance that focuses on an aesthetic look, also contributes to a pressure to be thin. Rarely is there only one cause for an eating disorder. Once an eating disorder is identified by family members or friends, an individual receives an immense amount of attention. However, many individuals with eating disorders are uncomfortable with the attention and believe they do not deserve the concern or costs associated with treatment. Given the secretive nature of eating disorders, it is erroneous to assume they are strategies for attention seeking. If you would like to read more about the complex causes of eating disorders please check out question #14.

3. IF A PERSON LOOKS NORMAL (READ "NOT TOO SKINNY"), THEN A PERSON DOESN'T HAVE AN EATING DISORDER

A common misconception is that someone must look a particular way to suffer from disordered eating. The belief that only emaciated and severely underweight individuals qualify for an eating disorder diagnosis is damaging and reflects a narrow view of eating disorders. In addition to the highly recognizable anorexia nervosa that involves severe restriction of food and accompanying weight loss, bulimia nervosa and binge eating disorder are associated with overeating behaviors. In fact, people who struggle from eating disorders represent a wide range of shapes, body weights, and sizes. It is accurate to associate anorexia nervosa, which is characterized by severe restriction of food, with rapid weight loss and low body mass index (BMI). However, individuals who engage in binge episodes of consuming large amounts of food may be overweight or obese. Many individuals who suffer from bulimia nervosa, which is characterized by binge episodes followed by an inappropriate compensatory method, will have a normal BMI. Interestingly, most eating disorders are difficult to detect from a person's physical appearance. Many individuals who struggle with eating disorders are a normal weight or slightly overweight, not ultra-thin. This misconception is damaging because people may be less likely to seek help if they do not fit the skinny stereotype associated with an eating disorder. It is also problematic because detection might be less likely in normal-weight individuals if people around them believe only skinny people suffer from eating disorders. Individuals who are in treatment, especially in group therapy, may struggle with thoughts about whether they are *sick enough* (meaning "thin enough") to fit into a group and to be deserving of treatment. Finally, this misconception can result in individuals suffering for years without treatment. To learn more about the characteristics of an eating disorder, see question #1.

4. PEOPLE GROW OUT OF EATING DISORDERS

It is a common belief that only teenagers worry about how they look. The myth that people graduate from eating disorders or outgrow body dissatisfaction has not been supported by research. One study found women in the United States aged 40–60 were the most dissatisfied age subgroup of all women. Although there is a misconception that as people mature they stop caring about the shape and size of their bodies, the reality is that the triggers remain in our weight-focused culture. Our sense of insecurity related to our body and its flaws lingers. The research suggests additional concerns, such as changes related to body weight and skin texture may contribute to a higher dissatisfaction in middle-aged individuals. Individuals cite wrinkles, increased hair growth in undesired areas, and weight gain as factors associated with aging directly related to life milestones that undermine positive body image. Although adolescents and college-aged individuals are considered at risk for eating disorders more than other age group, only 40 percent of eating disorders occur in people aged 15–19. A person of any age can suffer from a poor body image or develop an eating disorder. Some studies show women experience intense body dissatisfaction during certain life milestones such as pregnancy, giving birth, or menopause. Pregnancy may be associated with bodily changes that contribute to stretch marks, weight gain, or other conditions. Menopause may also contribute to body weight changes because of the increased storage of fat tissue and hormonal changes. People of all ages can be identified as struggling with negative body image and disordered eating behavior. Therefore, education is important so individual cases that fall outside of the adolescent age bracket are not overlooked To learn more about which groups of individuals may be most at risk for eating disorders, refer to question #11.

5. EATING DISORDERS ARE ONLY A FEMALE PROBLEM

A persistent misconception is that only girls and women have eating disorders. In reality, boys and men suffer from anorexia nervosa, bulimia nervosa, and binge eating disorder, as well as negative body image and body disturbances. Historically, research on eating disorders has focused on girls and young women, however, there is now some recognition that males face body image pressures too. Boys and men wanted to change their appearance, but instead of losing weight and becoming thinner, the male body ideal was hyper-masculine, incredibly muscular, and lean. Aligned with masculine toys of superhero and G.I. Joe action figures, male bodies were becoming increasingly more difficult to attain. This change is difficult to accomplish without a *clean diet*, intense workouts, supplementation of protein powders, and steroids. *Muscle dysmorphia* characterized males who wanted to gain weight and were experiencing intense dissatisfaction with their bodies. This body image condition (although not a formal eating disorder diagnosis) brought much-needed attention to the psychological concerns that boys and men have around their bodies. Given that negative body image is a key feature of an eating disorder, it follows that boys and men would logically suffer from them as well. One explanation for a lower rate of eating disorder prevalence in males relates to a tendency to under-report disordered eating behaviors. Further, boys and men who struggle with disordered eating patterns are less likely to seek treatment for an eating disorder and may be less likely to be diagnosed by a clinician even when displaying signs of disordered eating symptomatology. Moreover, research studies may be biased toward using measurements that were traditionally developed for girls and women that fail to capture the unique appearance-related demands for boys and men. Please see question #8 for more about the influence of sex on eating disorders.

QUESTIONS AND ANSWERS

Identification of Eating Disorders

1. What are the characteristics of an eating disorder?

Although eating disorders are most often recognized as a distinct change in eating patterns or body weight, it is important to remember that a disorder is complex; eating disorders are about much more than food or a number on a bathroom scale. These mental health disorders are symptomatic of a variety of psychological characteristics such as perfectionism, low self-esteem, hypersensitivity, and achievement orientation. Another key element of eating disorders is body image conflicts that manifest as distortions of one's size, such as seeing one's body as larger than it actually is or dissatisfaction with one's body shape, size, weight, musculature, or particular body parts. This dissatisfaction with one's body is predictive of associated disordered behaviors, such as restricting food intake and purging including vomiting and using laxatives or other compensatory methods. Disordered behaviors may begin in childhood, adolescence, or present for the first time in adulthood. Eating disorders occur in boys and girls, as well as men and women of all races and ethnic backgrounds.

Psychological Features

Individuals with eating disorders are commonly described as intelligent, high-achievers, and people-pleasers. As perfectionists, they set unrealistically high standards for themselves. These perfectionists strive to get the best grades, perform well in all sports, and do everything possible to be popular and well liked. Individuals with eating disorders are thought to have difficulty identifying and expressing internal emotions, which is termed *interoceptive awareness*. Individuals attempt to control emotions through their relationship with food. Some individuals with eating disorders, particularly people diagnosed with anorexia nervosa, are characterized as rigid, inflexible, and stubborn. These individuals are risk-averse and avoid conflicts in interpersonal relationships. Additionally, individuals with eating disorders may exhibit *maturity fears*, which refers to anxiety associated with growing older and becoming dependent.

By contrast, individuals diagnosed with bulimia nervosa are described as impulsive and likely to make risky decisions. They may experiment with alcohol and other drugs or be sexually promiscuous. Regardless of the type of eating disorder, people with eating disorders are typically individuals who successfully take care of other people but fall short of self-care. A distinguishing feature of individuals with eating disorders is a tendency to have poor self-esteem that is often linked to a negative body perception.

Body Image

Individuals with an eating disorder commonly suffer from negative body image and express intense dissatisfaction with their body shape, size, weight, or specific body parts (e.g., thighs, stomach, and nose). To this end, there is a tendency to agonize about changing particular aspects of appearance to address perceived body flaws. Body dissatisfaction has been identified as the strongest predictor for disordered eating. Eating disorders take shape in a variety of pathogenic methods to control or change one's body weight. Although clinical eating disorders are classified by explicit diagnostic criteria, disordered eating behaviors run the gamut from consuming an overly narrow diet; restricting calories; vomiting food; using laxatives, diet pills, or enemas; to overeating. Compensatory behavior can also take the form of excessive exercise to purge after overeating or to control emotions.

Trauma and Coexisting Disorders

Individuals with eating disorders experience a higher rate of trauma than the general population. This trauma may take the form of physical, sexual, or emotional abuse; however, not all individuals with eating disorders have been victims of trauma. In addition to having a relationship to trauma and post-traumatic stress disorder, eating disorders may coexist with other mental disorders, such as mood disorders (e.g., depression), anxiety disorders, obsessive-compulsive disorder, suicidality, and substance use disorders. Additionally, some individuals with eating disorders engage in self-harm, such as cutting, as a negative coping strategy. It is important to assess for a history of trauma, as well as suicidal thoughts and ideations. Trauma and coexisting disorders add a layer of complexity to identifying and treating individuals with eating disorders.

Signs and Symptoms to Look For

There are several signals that you, or someone you know, may have an eating disorder. Examine these questions as a starting point:

1. Body weight changes: have you or someone you know gained or lost a lot of weight in a short time?
2. Eating pattern changes: have you noticed a sudden change in eating habits? Has someone started a diet or adopted a vegetarian lifestyle without any explanation?
3. Exercise as priority: have you noticed an increased commitment to exercise or prioritization of exercise over other activities?
4. Comments about appearance: are you aware of frequent comments about appearance of self and others?
5. Presence of mood swings: have you observed mood swings that seem to come and go and are marked by extreme highs and lows?
6. Problems with sleep: have you noticed someone having problems with sleep, getting to sleep, or other sleep disturbances?
7. Social isolation: have you observed a tendency to become socially isolated and spend more time alone?
8. Secretive behavior: have you noticed large amounts of money are unaccounted for, or found excessive restaurant or grocery receipts? Have you interrupted someone you know who is eating secretively? Have you found fast-food wrappers or other evidence of a binge episode?
9. Hiding one's appearance: have you seen you or someone you know wearing baggy clothing to hide one's appearance, or discussing body flaws incessantly?
10. Evidence of purging: have you found laxatives, diuretics, diet pills, or some other medication that could be used for purging? Have you smelled vomit?
11. Changes in mood or anxiety: have you noticed the presence of depression, anxiety, or low self-esteem, especially when it was not obvious in the past?

It is important to remember that eating disorders are highly secretive in nature. Individuals go to extreme measures to hide behaviors. A person might give the appearance of eating regular meals with family to alleviate worry and concern, or he or she may try to hide vomiting after meals. Individuals with eating disorders tend to become more isolated and spend more time alone, as they become further entrenched in disordered eating patterns. For example, an individual who is increasingly compelled to exercise for longer periods may miss family or social obligations. Individuals with eating disorders may also find work and school responsibilities suffer. The types of eating disorders will be discussed in question 2 and include anorexia nervosa, bulimia nervosa, and binge eating disorder.

2. What are the different types of eating disorders?

Disordered eating exists on a spectrum with various types of eating behaviors that are not considered healthy. When disordered behaviors are identified, a mental health provider will assess for clinical eating disorders using specific diagnostic criteria. It is important, as part of this assessment process, to identify the type of eating disorder and evaluate the severity of symptoms to submit for insurance coverage for treatment; however, it is important to realize that disordered eating behaviors fall along a continuum. Even if an individual is considered subclinical (i.e., does not meet the clinical criteria for a medical diagnosis), there can still be negative health consequences, and treatment may be indicated. Moreover, disordered eating behaviors that fail to meet full clinical criteria may evolve into a full-fledged eating disorder over time.

Mental health providers use a common language for assessing eating disorders that is outlined by a published list of symptoms provided in the American Psychiatric Association's *Diagnostic Statistical Manual of Mental Disorders*. The most current version of this "clinician's bible" (i.e., *Diagnostic Statistical Manual for Mental Disorders, fifth edition* [DSM-5]) for diagnosing mental health disorders has revised the eating category disorder substantially. The formal categories of anorexia nervosa and bulimia nervosa have been retained, whereas Eating Disorder Not Otherwise Specified (EDNOS) has been omitted in the newest edition. EDNOS, which previously was used by clinicians to capture eating disorders that did not neatly fit into anorexia nervosa or bulimia nervosa as well as subclinical behaviors, became problematic as it turned into a "catchall" diagnosis. Therefore, the EDNOS categorization was changed to other specified feeding or eating disorder (OSFED). Unspecified feeding or eating disorder (UFED) can now be used to characterize individuals who fail to meet the typical eating disorder criteria but who present significant struggles with eating and food that warrant clinical attention. To add specificity in the fifth edition, binge eating disorder was added to diagnose individuals who present with binge symptoms without the use of purging methods. Another new addition to the *DSM-5* was the avoidant/restrictive food intake disorder (ARFID) as a diagnostic category. This diagnosis expands the previous diagnosis of feeding disorder of infancy or early childhood that may be unrelated to body image concerns.

Therefore, the current edition of the *DSM* identifies the following conditions within the eating disorder section: anorexia nervosa, bulimia nervosa, binge eating, and other feeding disorders (e.g., ARFID). These disorders will be defined in more detail here.

Anorexia Nervosa

The most recognizable eating disorder is anorexia nervosa (AN), which is characterized by being severely underweight as a result of limiting food intake. Sometimes, AN has been referred to as *self-starvation syndrome* to reflect the tendency to restrict the amount and type of foods consumed, so that the basic daily energy requirement is not met. Individuals with AN exhibit an intense fear of gaining weight and high anxiety around meals. Weight loss results in a malnourished or emaciated appearance, but individuals with AN show body distortion by typically overreporting their size and body weight. Negative body image is also a key feature; individuals with AN report high body dissatisfaction associated with perceived weight gain.

In the previous edition of the *Diagnostic Manual of Mental Disorders*, the criteria for a diagnosis of AN included loss of the menstrual cycle (i.e., amenorrhea); however, this criterion has been eliminated in recognition that males also suffer from AN. There are some variations of individuals who suffer from AN. The restricting type of AN involves weight loss through dieting, severe restriction or fasting, and/or the use of excessive exercise. The second subtype for AN involves purging episodes in the past three months, such as vomiting or binge eating behavior. The severity of the illness is based on an individual's body mass index (BMI), which is calculated using height and weight.

Bulimia Nervosa

The second formal category of eating disorder is bulimia nervosa (BN), which literally has been translated in Latin as *hunger of an ox*. This mental health disorder is best known for episodes of binge eating large amounts of food followed by the use of a compensatory method to eliminate the food. Binge eating often consists of rapidly consuming foods (within two hours) high in sugar, fat, and calories, resulting in intense emotions of guilt. The binge should be distinguished from holiday meals and would be much larger than what most individuals would eat in a defined period. Further, binge eating is characterized by a sense that one does not have control over eating, how much food is consumed, or the ability to stop. Binge eating is typically associated with stress or other intense emotions before and immediately after a binge episode.

The resultant guilt drives the desire to reverse the binge. Methods vary from abusing laxatives, diuretics (i.e., water pills), exercise, or induced vomiting. On average, the frequency of binge eating episodes and purging behaviors occurs at least once a week for several months.

Individuals with BN may be at a normal weight or slightly above or below what would be considered normal. However, these people experience intense body dissatisfaction and negative body image. In other words, one's sense of self-worth is tied to body shape and weight. The severity of BN is associated with the frequency of inappropriate compensatory behaviors, as well as other symptoms and level of daily functioning. Typically, mild BN is 1–3 purging episodes per week, moderate BN is 4–7 weekly episodes, severe BN is 8–13 episodes weekly, and extreme BN is 14 or more episodes per week.

Binge Eating Disorder

The newest formal category for eating disorders in the *DSM-5* is binge eating disorder (BED). BED represents a pattern of behavior marked by a struggle with recurring binge eating (or eating too much in one sitting) episodes. Essentially, binge eating episodes should occur at least once weekly for three months to receive a diagnosis of BED. Like BN, binge eating episodes involve ingesting large amounts of food (more than what is expected in a short period) in a discrete time frame (under two hours). Binge episodes are not synonymous with holiday meals. A key feature of BED is the tendency to experience feeling a lack of control over one's eating (i.e., inability to stop eating) during an episode. One is not able to appropriately redirect oneself from eating and is unable to control how much food is consumed. In some cases, binge eating episodes involve driving through multiple fast-food restaurants for food. Binge eaters prefer to be secretive about episodes and consume food in private.

A binge eating episode is generally associated with rapid eating and discomfort (too full) after a binge. Binge episodes may involve eating when not physically hungry (i.e., emotional eating). It is common for binge episodes to happen alone due to embarrassment or shame. Finally, it is likely that a person will experience disgust, depression, or guilt immediately after binging.

Unlike BN, a compensatory method is not typically used after an overeating episode for BED. This mental health disorder is the newest formal eating disorder diagnosis but was previously listed in the appendix of the fourth edition of the *DSM*. Due to large consumption of unhealthy foods, the tendency to gain weight or become overweight is likely. Therefore, BED likely represents a subgroup of overweight and obese individuals who are suffering from emotional eating and should be treated for an eating disorder.

It is important to reiterate that individuals with BED describe being out of control during binge episodes. Therefore, it is not helpful to tell someone with BED to "stop eating" or to prescribe him or her with a diet or meal plan. Like BN, binge foods such as potato chips, cookies, or ice cream often contain high calories, fat, and sugar and contribute to intense guilt. Binge episodes are tied to intense emotional experiences and vary in frequency. Severity of BED is characterized by the number of episodes per week: Mild BED is characterized by 1–3 weekly episodes, moderate BED is 4–7 weekly episodes, severe BED is 8–13 weekly episodes, and extreme BED is 14 or more weekly binge eating episodes.

Avoidant/Restrictive Food Intake Disorder

Avoidant/restrictive food intake disorder (ARFID) represents a new disorder in the eating disorder section of the *DSM-5*. ARFID is characterized by dysfunctional eating behaviors, such as food restriction, that lead to severe nutritional deficiencies. Although these deficits likely result in unhealthy weight loss, they are not tied to body image disturbances or dieting for appearance reasons. This disorder can be found in both children and adults and has been linked to traumatic experiences (e.g., choking) and other disorders, such as autism spectrum disorders and attention deficit disorder.

People with ARFID are unable to meet the daily requirements for food intake or to receive the quality of food consumption as recommended by the United States Department of Agriculture (USDA) due to severe food restriction behavior. Dietary restraint may be associated with certain food aversions related to the smell, texture, or taste of the item. Other contributing factors include emotional problems associated with eating and food phobias such as fear of choking. ARFID affects both children and adults. In children, ARFID looks very different from both anorexia and bulimia. However, in adults, ARFID shares several important characteristics with anorexia. Importantly, a common set of symptoms should be assessed for ARFID to determine whether there is a problem.

Assessing for ARFID involves checking for significant weight loss, medical signs of nutritional deficiencies, or significant impairment in psychosocial functioning. Individuals who suffer from ARFID may also rely heavily on medically administered feeding (e.g., enteral feeding) or oral supplements rather than getting their caloric intake through whole foods. Children with ARFID may exhibit a failure to meet expected growth markers and weight gain that are considered healthy for their age.

ARFID relates to (and is sometimes confused with) similarly restrictive eating behaviors, such as picky eating, but is considered a separate condition. *Selective eating disorder*, which is often used to label picky eaters, conforms to this tendency to refuse certain types of food and to restrict food based on a variety of reasons. The distinction is that selective eating disorder is not typically characterized by extreme growth deficiencies or nutritional problems. Furthermore, to meet the clinical diagnosis for ARFID, behavior should not be explained by any existing medical condition (e.g., gastrointestinal distress). It is important to underscore that food restriction is not tied to body image or desire to lose weight. Finally, having access to food due to socioeconomic status should not play a factor in causing the restrictive behavior to be classified as ARFID.

3. What is the difference between disordered eating and an eating disorder?

It is important to understand the differences between *disordered eating* and *eating disorder*. First, an eating disorder generally has a formal diagnosis that aligns with specific clinical criteria for AN, BN, or BED. This formal diagnosis is often required for insurance to reimburse treatment for eating disorders. Second, an eating disorder tends to be more severe and extreme than disordered eating behaviors. Finally, a real eating disorder is usually associated with lack of functioning in a number of areas. An individual with an eating disorder may experience physical consequences as evidenced by sleep disturbances. Socially, an individual with an eating disorder might experience consequences like mood swings, irritability, or depression. Effects on social life may be present for someone with an eating disorder, including conflicts with family members or isolation from friends. Work or sport performance may suffer as well.

Disordered eating represents a broad range of behaviors often associated with clinical eating disorders. Certain groups, such as teens or athletes, may normalize disordered eating behaviors as dieting strategies. This is dangerous because adolescents may actually learn behaviors (e.g., how to purge) from each other. With the emergence of social media, this challenge has increased. Websites, blogs, and discussion forums promoting weight loss have proliferated and offer both healthy and unhealthy weight control strategies.

To illustrate this point: 62 percent of female adolescents admitted to following disordered eating behaviors to lose weight. Behaviors include restriction of certain foods or obsessive calorie monitoring, calorie counting, or calorie cutting. Additional disordered eating behaviors include compensatory methods, such as vomiting or abusing laxatives, enemas, or diet pills. Excessive and compulsive exercise, another disordered eating behavior, may also be used to purge. Binge eating episodes characterized by overeating and being out of control represent yet another disordered eating behavior.

Disordered eating behaviors are also a way to manipulate body weight for sport competition. Athletes, such as wrestlers or boxers, who do not necessarily meet the full clinical criteria for an eating disorder, may elect to engage in pathogenic weight loss strategies to meet sport-related weight limits and weigh-in goals or to change weight class. Changing food intake by restricting or purging may be viewed as a way to enhance performance.

The primary distinction between disordered eating behaviors and eating disorders is severity. While a clinical eating disorder must meet identified diagnostic criteria, disordered eating does not satisfy the full criteria. Disordered eating, which is often referred to as a *subclinical* eating disorder, may reflect pathogenic behaviors that are used less frequently than the criteria or present at a lower severity than a full-blown eating disorder. However, it is important that all disordered eating behaviors be taken seriously. First, disordered eating behavior has been shown to lead to more severe clinical eating disorders if left untreated. Disordered eating has also been linked to the future development of other mental disorders such as anxiety disorder or mood disorders (e.g., depression). Moreover, individuals who engage in disordered eating behaviors can suffer from deleterious

health consequences. Therefore, they may experience lasting effects from
behaviors that seemed harmless and normal at the time.

4. What are orthorexia nervosa and selective eating?

Although the general population is encouraged to consume more fruits
and vegetables to meet the USDA nutritional guidelines, eating too much
or too little can result in an imbalance or *yo-yo* dieting. Moreover, taking
healthy eating too far can result in a condition that has been dubbed *orthorexia nervosa*. Orthorexia nervosa is distinct from other eating disorders
in that individuals do not obsess about body weight, rather they place
undue emphasis on the perceived quality of food.

The condition of orthorexia nervosa is characterized as an obsessive fixation on eating only healthy foods that are considered pure. In
some cases, this focus centers around eating organic foods and avoiding
artificial colors, genetically modified foods, or preservatives. Someone
with orthorexia nervosa may also avoid all dairy and animal products
or other types of food, such as sugar or salt. This preoccupation with
eating healthy leads to the avoidance of foods perceived as harmful. The
term, which came from the Greek *orthos* meaning "correct," was coined
in 1996 to refer to an obsession with a narrow diet to include so-called
healthy foods. This condition is distinct from other formal types of eating
disorders identified in the *DSM-5* and does not have formal diagnostic
criteria. However, it is recognized that this fixation parallels other eating
disorders.

Individuals with orthorexia nervosa may demonstrate a variety of
behavior changes as a result of their condition. For example, there may
be the tendency to attribute the avoidance of certain types of food to a
specific food allergy that is unsupported by medical diagnosis. There may
be increased use of nutritional supplements, as well as herbal remedies
that represent a preference for *natural* products. Dietary choice becomes
increasingly narrow for individuals with orthorexia. It is common for
individuals to limit their diets to less than 10 acceptable food choices.
They demonstrate an obsessive concern about food and health concerns.
Finally, individuals with this condition will likely develop strong concern
for how foods are prepared, including the washing of foods and sterilizing
of utensils. Additional barriers result in reduced food intake and inflexibility around meal environments.

Given this increased obsession and narrowing of food choices, individuals with orthorexia nervosa experience changes in activities of daily living. They may avoid social events that involve food, which may result in social isolation or alienation from friends or family members. Some individuals with orthorexia nervosa experience emotional distress associated with their obsession around food. In extreme cases, individuals may suffer from panic attacks or intense anxiety. Mood swings, depression, and irritability may also result from orthorexia nervosa. Guilt may arise from disappointing others or from eating a forbidden food. Thinking about food becomes all-encompassing for an individual with orthorexia nervosa and takes over life. Unfortunately, this obsession leads to intense food planning around future meals. Food satisfaction is undermined due to negative thoughts around food choices.

Selective eating refers to the eating pattern of children or adults who will only eat an extremely narrow range of foods. Family members experience frustration with the apparent rigidity of behavior, despite encouragement or threat of punishment. Some foods that selective eaters may choose include peanut butter, white bread with no crust, pizza, steak, and pasta (with or without sauce). More research is needed to understand selective eating disorder; however, several trends have been identified. Selective eating tends to run in families. It is also more common in boys than girls. Generally, the medical response to selective eating disorder in children is physical examination. A physician can use growth charts to evaluate whether growth is at a normal pace.

5. Is an eating disorder actually a food phobia, or is that something else entirely?

Sometimes having a direct fear of food may be mistaken for selective eating, picky eating, or anorexia nervosa; however, it is important to note that the technical term *food phobia* refers to a separate condition and is more generalized to all eating rather than limited to certain types of foods. Although a person with an eating disorder may present with anxiety and fear around food, a food *phobia* represents a distinct phenomenon that is not well understood in the pediatric community. Medical causes or conditions should be ruled out that could contribute to food phobia that could explain aversion to eating or poor food intake. This food restriction or inability to eat is not associated with body image concerns, a desire to lose weight, or to attain a particular body type.

Typically, a patient with a food phobia will display a refusal of food (especially solid food) and may not swallow anything, including saliva. Examples include foods that are lumpy in texture that pose a potential choking hazard or type of food that has shells or bone. Although food phobia is referred to as *functional dysphagia* to explain the potential experience relative to a fear of swallowing, a food phobia may also involve fears related to vomiting, experiencing abdominal pain, or suffocating. The condition can start at a very young age or can occur in adulthood. Meals can represent an anxiety-provoking event due to these extreme fears. Children may also face risks for being bullied for their food restrictive behaviors and not eating the same foods as everyone else.

For individuals who are presenting with food aversions that take place over an extended period of time and are not attributable to medical conditions or negative body image, the *DSM-5* diagnosis of avoidant/restrictive food intake disorder (AFRID) can be given. A family history of anxiety disorders is suspected for food phobias.

Although more research is needed to explain the origin of this food phobia, children report that their food refusal is attributed to a fear of choking, vomiting, or germ contamination (that could result in illness). They believe food and water will lodge in their throats. In some cases, children are unwilling to discuss reasons for not eating or drinking. Onset of the food phobia is often sudden and linked to an incident of choking or witnessing a choking episode.

6. Is an eating disorder an addiction? Is there such a thing as being addicted to food?

Many experts argue that there is no such thing as a food addiction. From a clinical perspective, food addiction has not been included in the *DSM-5*, meaning that there are no official criteria for a diagnosis.

Despite the debate around food addiction, eating disorders have sometimes been associated with addictive behavior. The relationship between disordered eating and addiction aligns with the compulsion to behave in a particular way, such as restricting or purging food. This behavior is accompanied with an intense sense of being unable to control self. Additionally, the idea that people experience intense food cravings in a similar way that individuals crave other substances supports that food addiction exists.

Food cravings have been described as an intense urge to consume a specific type of food. Usually this craving seems to come out of nowhere, is extremely strong, and seems impossible to satiate without eating the food of obsession. Many food cravings have been found to affect one's mood and may be triggered when certain emotions (e.g., stress, frustration, anger) are present. Experiencing a strong urge to consume a particular food item has also been shown to correlate with a tendency to overeat due to a person's inability to recognize biological cues of hunger and fullness. Interestingly, there are valid biological explanations for food cravings linked to brain chemistry.

One example of a common source of food craving is sugar. Sugar is found in both natural food sources (e.g., fruits) and processed items and is believed to contain chemical properties that affect the brain. In this case, sugar or glucose creates a high or rush often followed by a sharp crash, similar to a drug. It is believed certain foods, like sugar, trigger sensations in the brain providing an immediate reward that mimics addictive drugs like cocaine.

Paradoxically the research shows that when people have deprived themselves of certain foods they believe are "bad," they may be more vulnerable to eat larger amounts of food or engage in a binge episode. The binge behavior of sugary foods can result in creating a vicious cycle. Sugar releases opioids and dopamine in the brain, and studies have discovered that rats can become dependent on sugar. Naturally, this same addictive tendency likely occurs in humans. Brain chemistry plays a critical role in addiction, and neuroscientists have been diligent to better understand the neural pathways and what happens when animals and humans ingest certain foods like sugar. Therefore, evidence for possible chemical dependence on sugar and other food items may support further research and the identification of a formal diagnosis for food addiction.

Food as addiction and food cravings have been depicted in the media and are commonly accepted. Chocolate has been identified as the most popular food craving in Western society. Its popularity as an object of craving makes sense given that it is dense in carbohydrates, as well as fat and protein. A biological explanation for chocolate cravings is that chocolate contains cocoa and is thought to induce mood-enhancing neurotransmitters in the brain.

Although food addiction is not a formal eating disorder and is not included as a clinical diagnosis, more research is needed to understand food cravings and the addictive qualities of food. Importantly, the link of brain chemistry to eating patterns shows promise in the identification and treatment of food addiction and eating disorders. Understanding eating patterns related to psychological or physical cravings may be useful for health promotion and obesity prevention. Because having intense food cravings and a sense of powerlessness over certain foods can cause overeating episodes, there are concerns that experiencing a food or sugar addiction will lead directly to weight gain or obesity.

7. How can eating disorders be detected?

Eating disorders may be identified in a number of ways depending on the age of a person and the type of disordered eating. For example, school-aged children may be weighed for BMI reports, typically for the purpose of tracking weight and identifying obesity. For individuals who have gained or lost weight, this report, when read by parents, may trigger recognition of weight-related changes. Teachers or school counselors may also notice changes in mood or behaviors in students. It is also likely that friends may become concerned about a classmate and bring it to the attention of a teacher or parent. Medical providers, at all levels, are more aware of eating disorders and vigilant about dramatic weight changes in children and adolescents.

Although eating disorders are sometimes detected during an annual visit with a pediatrician or a physician, this is the exception not the rule. A medical professional who may detect an eating disorder is a dentist. It is more common for a family dentist to identify dental issues and gum problems with a potential eating disorder, especially with the association to purging behavior found in individuals with bulimia nervosa.

In many cases, a family member, friend, or someone who knows the person will notice changes in eating behaviors and mood. For example, the family member may notice a sudden shift in a teenager's willingness to eat red meat or animal products. In other instances, rapid weight loss is observed along with a sickly appearance. Another possibility is watching a male or female family member suddenly adopt a rigid exercise regimen that takes priority over all other responsibilities (work, school, and social). Other behavioral changes may include going to the bathroom frequently after meals or refusing to eat certain items on the plate. Finally, disordered eating may begin with dieting behavior. Eating patterns might start as a purported attempt to eat healthier or eat less dessert before becoming a regimented meal plan.

Frequently, these physical or behavioral changes are accompanied by mood changes. A person who is struggling from disordered eating or an eating disorder may appear depressed or anxious, or demonstrate volatile mood changes. There may be some other changes such as decreased interest in social activities and academic endeavors, or decreased performance in sport. In athletics, a coach or athletic trainer might notice that an athlete is more irritable or is exhibiting changes in dietary habits or training behavior. Athletic trainers, who are often on the front line, may also spot sudden weight changes in athletes engaged in disordered eating.

Regardless of who observes the changes or unhealthy behaviors, it is important to gently confront an individual who is potentially struggling. Using "I" statements is preferable to putting a person on the defensive. Reinforcing in a caring way that one is concerned is more likely to be well received than statements like "you don't eat anything anymore" or "you need to eat." Generally, having a conversation about observations related to changes will be met with resistance and perhaps denial. However, the goal is to assist the individual to seek help and eventually treatment. If no one says anything, the individual will likely continue down the disordered eating path, so it is important to introduce and support treatment and recovery.

Assessment of eating disorders can be done in a variety of ways. In a research setting, questionnaires often assess eating disorder risk. In a treatment setting, clinical interviews and questionnaires are commonly used to assess disordered eating thoughts and behaviors. Treatment professionals, such as counselors and social workers, conduct assessments for eating disorders at a specialty eating disorder or mental health clinic that typically requires an in-depth interview. A counselor asks a variety of questions to understand whether an individual is exhibiting signs and symptoms of an eating disorder. Treatment professionals also want to get a sense of coexisting conditions and will assess for depression, anxiety, or other mood disorders, as well as substance use. In addition, they may ask questions about self-harming, suicidal thoughts, or a history of trauma.

It is commonly agreed that seeking treatment voluntarily is more successful than being involuntarily committed to treatment. Therefore, an assessment is merely a starting point to determine what level of care (inpatient, residential, partial hospitalization, outpatient) is most appropriate. An assessment can also be useful for allowing a person to voice eating disorder struggles and can be the first step toward recovery.

8. Can boys and men get eating disorders? What is muscle dysmorphia?

There is a stereotype that girls and women have eating disorders and that boys and men are immune from developing an eating disorder. Unfortunately, eating disorders do not discriminate when it comes to gender. Although eating disorders have often been viewed as a *female disease*, boys and men also suffer from disordered eating and eating disorders. Historically, there is evidence that boys and men face more intense pressure regarding unrealistic body ideals. One example is the G.I. Joe figure that shifted from being an *average Joe* to an action figure with bulging muscles and well-defined V-shaped upper body. Eating disorder clinicians have reported seeing male clients as young as nine years old, and the ratio of clients with eating disorder has purportedly changed from 19 to 1 (female to male clients) to 9 to 1 (female to male clients) at one major medical center. Most commonly, male clients are expected to be 10 percent of all eating disorder cases. Prevalence statistics vary across studies, but a 2007 report indicated that among men, 0.3 percent had anorexia nervosa, 0.5 percent had bulimia nervosa, and 2 percent had binge eating disorder at some point in their lives.

Given that both boys and girls are inundated with images in the media advertising the perfect body, it is not surprising that both sexes face pressure to change their physiques, even if they strive for different ideal body types. Male models depicted in magazines, commercials, and Internet advertisements have extremely low body fat, perfectly sculpted biceps, and *six-pack abs*. Whether these images are airbrushed or photoshopped, they serve as inspiration for boys and men to change their bodies. For example, for males the desirable body type may be represented by the masculine ideal of muscularity, strength, and power in contrast to the female's ideal body of femininity and ultra-thin. Boys and men may also report wanting to get larger rather than smaller (at least where muscle is concerned), but the desire to change is the common denominator for males and females. When a change becomes an obsession, it is time to notice.

Many boys and men attempt to gain muscle by lifting weights and engaging in intensive exercise regimens. However, the terms *muscle dysmorphia* and *bigorexia* were coined in 1993 by Harrison Pope, Jr., who is a psychiatric researcher at Harvard University. Pope studied steroid use in weight lifters and noticed a pattern of anorexic tendencies that seemed to occur in a reverse direction. The characteristics of weight lifters, including the presence of compulsive and excessive exercise, seemed to mirror what was seen in clients with anorexia nervosa. Muscle dysmorphia was considered a subtype of body dysmorphic disorder (i.e., clinically, obsession with a particular body part, such as one's nose). However, muscle dysmorphia featured a preoccupation and obsession with one's muscle size rather than a specific body part for boys and men. This obsession was associated with an excessive desire to have a larger body size, increased muscles, and higher body dissatisfaction. This dysfunctional condition contrasted with a normative culture that promotes healthy and gradual body-related changes, due to the negative body image that is pervasive among individuals with muscle dysmorphia. It is important to note that boys and men who suffer from muscle dysmorphia, which has been labeled *reverse anorexia*, demonstrate the dysfunctional nature of the condition and exhibit body image disturbances with distortions regarding their muscles being too small, scrawny, and weak. Males with muscle dysmorphia underreport their size; females with anorexia nervosa overreport their size. Boys and men who had muscle dysmorphia were found to hide their appearance in baggy clothing and to camouflage perceived flaws with makeup or other clothing tricks. It was important for clinicians and researchers to understand that although males do not necessarily want to lose weight or become thinner, they report pressure to have a muscular physique. Bodybuilders and other male athletes often exhibit muscle dysmorphia, which exemplifies the dysfunctional body image that boys and men may face.

Although the sex bias associated with eating disorders continues to persist today, both boys and girls, as well as men and women, develop disordered eating patterns. It has been estimated that approximately 1 of 10 eating disorder cases is a male; however, there is suspicion that this number may be artificially low due to underreporting and missed diagnoses. First, general practitioners still believe that eating disorders are primarily a female condition. This stereotype may result in a medical practitioner being less likely to screen a boy or man for an eating disorder. Some of the typical signs such as loss of menstrual cycle are not relevant for male patients. Medical professionals might also be less likely to diagnose a male patient with anorexia nervosa, bulimia nervosa, or binge eating disorder, even when symptoms are present. In addition to the bias inherent in the medical community, publicity around eating disorders in the media and other public venues primarily focuses on girls and women. Therefore, family members of male individuals struggling with an eating disorder may be less likely to detect a problem and associate it with this disorder. Finally, a male client suffering from an eating disorder may experience shame or not think he should receive treatment for a condition ripe with sex-related stereotypes.

This stigma against male clients with eating disorders has disturbing effects. Unfortunately, males are less likely to seek treatment for eating disorders. In fact, a study found that only 16 percent of men with eating disorders, compared to 52 percent of women with eating disorders, received treatment. It is expected this disparity reflects a sense that it is not socially acceptable for boys and men to have an eating disorder. There is also a stereotype that boys with eating disorders are gay. However, studies have found that both straight and gay males can suffer from an eating disorder.

When boys and men finally do reach out for help, the eating disorder is often more severe because of the delay to seek treatment. These individuals may require a higher level of care, such as an inpatient or residential setting to address medical complications or lack of stability and functioning. Treatment is made difficult for this group as there are fewer treatment options available for boys and men with eating disorders. This inequity of available treatment choices may result in male clients having to accept an inappropriate level of care, traveling long distance to seek treatment, and spending more on care. Insurance companies may also be less likely to reimburse to keep males in treatment, given that the absence of menstrual cycle reduces the number of required medical markers for diagnosis.

The complexities of seeking and receiving care for men are compounded by the reality that certain males are more at risk for developing disordered eating behaviors. Certain athletes have been identified as one at-risk group. Specifically, sports like wrestling and boxing that involve weight classes trigger certain athletes to *suck weight* to improve performance. Other sports, like football, are associated with a pressure to gain weight and increase muscle mass. Players may be encouraged to eat more food and may struggle with unhealthy weight gain. One study found that 60 percent of National Football League players were overweight or obese as determined by their BMIs. Male bodybuilders, who focus on the appearance of muscles and body shape, have also shown a tendency toward disordered eating to become lean while building muscle.

9. How many people in the United States have eating disorders?

It is estimated that 20 million women and 10 million men suffer from a clinical eating disorder in the United States. These individuals meet the diagnostic criteria for anorexia nervosa, bulimia nervosa, or binge eating disorder. This number has risen substantially over the past several decades.

Unfortunately, it is extremely difficult to measure the prevalence of eating disorders for several reasons. First, eating disorders are underreported and often untreated, which means numerous individuals suffer without being diagnosed. Because eating disorders are kept a secret, individuals often experience intense shame and will not admit there is a problem. When these same individuals are confronted by friends and family members about observed changes and unhealthy behaviors, they will usually deny there is a problem and go out of their way to demonstrate normal eating. Second, for the cases that exist, reporting presents challenges. Not all private practitioners use *DSM-5* diagnoses, particularly for clients who pay out of pocket. There is not a centralized reporting system for diagnoses of eating disorder in the United States, which makes it challenging to maintain national prevalence data. Statistics by state are hard to obtain given that treatment settings range from schools to community clinics, as well as specialty treatment options to serve clients. Support groups for overeating and eating disorders are available across the United States but are intended to be anonymous, and participants are not tracked for population health research purposes.

10. Are eating disorders a problem only in the Western, industrialized world?

Eating disorders exist around the globe and are not limited to the United States. Although body ideals differ according to cultural norms across ethnic groups and countries of origin, the presence of body dissatisfaction, low self-esteem, and desire to change one's body are the common denominators. Factors such as frequency and type of media presence and availability or scarcity of food sources influence body image in a culture.

For example, in developing areas, such as sub-Saharan Africa or the Philippines, food security is not a given. In many countries, having a thin physique is viewed negatively and is associated with malnourishment and higher likelihood of diseases. By contrast, Western countries like the United States spend billions of dollars on dieting and diet products annually. Body image dissatisfaction exists across Europe with the fashion industry in Milan criticized for waiflike, anorexic-looking models. This has resulted in some countries' (e.g., Spain, Italy, and Israel) attempts to ban anorexic models from the catwalks with the passing of laws such as the French anorexic rule. Specifically, France has worked to outlaw excessively thin models, address individuals who have a BMI lower than 18.5, and require all models to produce a medical certificate stating they are healthy enough to work.

The prevalence of eating disorders is reported to be the lowest in Germany and the Netherlands. Europe, France, Italy, and Belgium have the highest eating disorder rates. Japan and other Asian countries are also at risk. Japan, for example, is largely influenced by the Western models and body ideals using Caucasian features as the beauty ideal. Efforts to become more Western-looking by having cosmetic surgery to change the shape of the nose or eyes are increasingly common. Moreover, dieting behavior has been shown even from a young age among 20–30 percent of Japanese youth, who are thought to lead the prevalence of eating disorder in Asian countries. It is estimated that 25–31 percent of female adolescents aged 13–29 have eating disorders.

China is more influenced by Western media now than in the past. Historically, there has been strong evidence of invasive efforts to change a female's body part (i.e., feet). Specifically, the practice of foot binding was used to inhibit growth, because smaller feet were considered to be more highly desirable for females in China. Other countries that have documented eating disorders and body dissatisfaction are Singapore, Taiwan, Pakistan, Malaysia, India, Thailand, and South Korea.

Africa is a diverse continent, with a rich history of admiring a curvaceous and overweight frame characterized by *meat on the bones*; today, people in Africa are not immune from eating disorders. In Ghana, for example, 1.5 percent of female adolescents were reported to be underweight due to restrictive eating associated with perfectionistic attitudes, low self-efficacy, and religious fasting. By contrast, men in Ghana sensed a pressure to be more muscular, symbolic of prestige and greater attractiveness. Senegal has recently received more Western media exposure. There is evidence of women in Senegal desiring to be thinner and having lighter skin. They reported using chemical skin bleaches, which can increase the risk of skin cancer, to achieve the light colored skin tone. Women in South Africa have also been increasingly more likely to experience pressure to be thin with the insurgence of the Western media.

South America is considered a hotbed for eating disorders. Brazil is the cosmetic surgery capital of the world with the highest rate of cosmetic surgery procedures. People from around the globe travel to Brazil to receive breast enhancement or reduction, liposuction, tummy tucks, and face lifts. Body image concerns and eating disorder symptoms, such as fasting and the use of laxatives and diuretics, have also appeared in Mexico. There is suspicion that this shift from a traditional heavy body type to a thinner body type is tied to an internalization of the thin Western ideal. In conclusion, regardless of the geographic location or cultural body ideal, the role of Western media can negatively influence the body image of people in other countries through exposure to unrealistic images. Likewise, disordered eating and eating disorders are becoming more evident in developing countries.

11. Are certain people more likely than others to develop an eating disorder?

Although eating disorders affect everyone regardless of age, sex, race, and socioeconomic class, certain trends have emerged with regard to demographic characteristics. These observed patterns have, in some cases, led to overgeneralized stereotypes (e.g., only females suffer from eating disorders) and should be used to understand at-risk groups rather than to make assumptions about who may have a problem.

Sex and Eating Disorder Risk

It is common for a person to automatically conjure an image of a young woman when visualizing a person with an eating disorder. Without question, there is a higher prevalence of eating disorder cases that involve female clients than their male counterparts. Historically, much more attention has been paid to girls and women in the literature, as well as in treatment settings. Approximately 30 million individuals in the United States are expected to suffer from eating disorders at some time in their life. Of these individuals, 10 million represent men who are much less likely to report or be diagnosed with eating disorders. One study found that the prevalence of anorexia nervosa over the lifetime is estimated to be 0.9 percent for women and 0.3 percent for men. The lifetime prevalence of bulimia nervosa and binge eating disorder for men is estimated to be 0.5 percent and 2 percent, respectively. Another related statistic is that women are three times more likely to develop an eating disorder.

It is likely that prevalence rates will change now that the most recent version of the *DSM* (i.e., *DSM-5* has eliminated the requirement for loss of menstrual cycle from the anorexia nervosa diagnostic criteria. Interestingly, one 2001 study indicated that the prevalence of males with eating disorders has increased. Over 20 years ago, males represented 1 case for every 10–15 female cases of eating disorders. At the time of the study, males were expected to represent one in every four cases of anorexia nervosa. However, males with eating disorders are much less likely to seek treatment. Only 16 percent of boys and men went for treatment as compared with 52 percent of females suffering from an eating disorder. This low treatment participation rate contributes to less knowledge and a continued perpetuation of this stereotype.

Further, because females have been historically considered higher risk than their male counterparts, boys and men have received much less attention in treatment and prevention efforts. Research studies have been devoid of male participants or have asked questions with a bias toward female body image concerns (e.g., smaller thighs). Treatment centers have catered their programming to the needs of female clients, and many do not admit male clients with eating disorders. Although this trend is slowly changing, much more work is done to understand the development and treatment of eating disorders among both sexes. Among male individuals with eating disorders, gay males and athletes from certain sports tend to exhibit more risk.

LGBTQI and Eating Disorder Risk

Although there is a paucity of eating disorder research that addresses sexuality and eating disorders, there is evidence that some segments of the LBGTQI population may face more risk for development of disordered eating. One at-risk group has been gay males, who have been shown to be more focused on their appearance and bodies than their straight counterparts. Although homosexuality alone is not attributed to eating disorder development, the psychological and sociocultural factors within the gay culture can contribute to increase the likelihood of behaviors. For example, several studies have noted the intense emphasis on attractiveness with a desire to have a fit and lean appearance among gay males. From a psychological perspective, gay males were found to score higher on femininity than straight males, which was associated with higher levels of body dissatisfaction.

Further, some studies suggest that LBGTQI populations are especially vulnerable for unique stressors in the workplace, school, and social settings. For example, harassment and being bullied are commonly reported, as well as increased vulnerability to anxiety, depression, and substance abuse. This predisposition to stress can contribute to an increased risk for disordered eating behaviors as an unhealthy coping mechanism. That is, eating disorders can be the direct result of the desire to control something (i.e., food) in one's life and a way to manage stress.

Despite the fact that gay males have been identified as an at-risk group, it is important to note that the associated myth that all males with eating disorders are gay can be damaging. Specifically, this assumption around sexuality may discourage heterosexual boys and men to seek treatment for their concern.

Age and Eating Disorder Risk

Eating disorders are likely to manifest themselves from an early age. While eating disorders have no minimum or maximum, it has been reported that an overwhelming number (80%) of 10-year-old girls have dieted. Purportedly, 40 to 60 percent of children between the ages of 6 and 12 are concerned about their body weight. Around 70 percent of them wanted to lose weight in order to slim down. Among 13-year-old girls, 53 percent expressed dissatisfaction with how their bodies look, and by 17 years of age, 78 percent have negative body image. Dieting and desire to lose weight are significant risk factors for disordered eating and eating disorders. Specifically, body dissatisfaction is the strongest predictor of one's tendency to develop an eating disorder.

A myth surrounding eating disorders is that only adolescents suffer from eating disorders. There is also the misguided perception that people magically outgrow negative body image. For anorexia nervosa, young women are most likely to develop this disorder between 15 and 24 years of age. One study reported that the median age for having an eating disorder ranges from 18 to 21; however, this number may not show the early developing disordered eating thoughts and behaviors that are reflected by dieting and body image concerns. The other problem with limiting attention to teens is that studies have found women from 40 to 60 years of age were more dissatisfied with their bodies than their younger (i.e., 20–39) or older (i.e., 60–79) counterparts. A separate study revealed that 67 percent of women over 30 years of age expressed strong body dissatisfaction. Alarmingly, when examining only women older than 65 years of age, the majority (60%) wanted to lose weight. Women enduring bodily changes associated with life milestones such as pregnancy and menopause reported negative body image and higher risk despite not falling into the stereotypical age bracket for eating disorder development.

The equally harmful assumption that younger children are protected from disordered eating behaviors or negative body image is pervasive. Alarmingly, young girls have been found to engage in dieting behavior at much younger ages. In fact, a vast majority (80%) of 10-year-old girls have been on a diet. The National Eating Disorder Association reported that approximately 40 to 60 percent of 6- to 12-year-old youth were worried about their weight. Within this age group 70 percent indicated wanting to lose weight. Among 13-year-old girls, over half of these tweens reported feeling dissatisfied with their bodies.

Ethnicity and Eating Disorder Risk

Eating disorders have traditionally been considered to be a disease of white privilege; however, this mental health disorder does not discriminate by race or ethnicity. Early studies included only Caucasian individuals, and more research is needed to fully understand eating disorder risk factors surrounding ethnicity. Despite the stereotypic image of eating disorders being a "white disease," it is not uncommon for people of color to struggle with disordered eating issues. To a large extent, the prevalence rate has been skewed by who is more likely to seek treatment for their problem. Individuals who self-identify as Hispanic, black, or Asian were reported to make fewer doctor visits and be less likely to carry insurance than their white counterparts. These trends result in less documentation of eating disorder cases among non-white individuals, which was estimated to be 3 to 5 percent for persons of color for clinics specialized in treating eating disorders.

Although the body image ideal may vary by culture or ethnic group, the common factor across groups seems to be a desire to change one's physique. For African American women, one study revealed that an ideal of having curvy hips with a tiny waist was considered ideal. Despite not being the overly thin ideal characterized in the Western media, this body type was still considered difficult to achieve. The dissatisfaction with one's body and the desire to lose weight can put Asians, Hispanics, and Caucasians equally at risk for disordered eating behaviors. Specifically, in one study 31.9 to 36.1 percent of these ethnicities reported they had tried to lose weight. Interestingly, an even higher prevalence of Native Americans (48%) had attempted to lose weight. This high tendency was reinforced in a separate study that found Native American teenagers, 48 percent of girls and 30 percent of boys, had dieted over the past year. Purging behavior was reported by 28 percent of Native American girls and 21 percent of Native American boys.

Another ethnicity thought to be susceptible for developing eating disorders has been Asians and Asian Americans. Asians were found to subscribe to the overly thin ideal of Western media and were likely to engage in behaviors to change themselves to meet this ideal; however, Asians were also less likely to seek treatment for their eating disorders because counseling was not acceptable in their culture. Asian girls were found to be more dissatisfied with their bodies and had lower self-esteem than their white counterparts, which puts them at increased risk for eating disorder development.

Athletes and Eating Disorder Risk

Sport participation has been identified as a potential risk factor; however, the data is mixed when it comes to the question of whether athletes are at a higher risk for developing eating disorders. On the one hand, sports can be a positive vehicle to teach values like teamwork; working hard; and building self-esteem to children, adolescents, and adults. However, certain sports can emphasize the advantage of having a certain body type in order to be more competitive. Therefore, coaches may encourage athletes to gain or lose weight depending on the sport or position a person is playing. Furthermore, certain sports may have formal weight requirements to try out for the sport or consistent weigh-ins throughout the season. For sports such as wrestling and boxing that involve weight classes to compete, athletes will face decisions about whether to lose weight to be more competitive in a lower weight class.

The prevalence data around athletes and eating disorder tends to be heavily influenced by which sports are included in the study. One study found that athletes were less likely to engage in dieting or be concerned about their weight than non-athletes. However, several studies have found that athletes in sports that are heavily focused on body weight and appearance may be more at risk for developing disordered eating behaviors than non-athletes or athletes in sports less focused on one's physique. Specifically, sports have been labeled *leanness-demand* if they possess characteristics that reinforce body shape, weight, or aesthetics of physique. For example, gymnastics and diving are characterized as aesthetic sports due to revealing team uniform, tendency to promote a lean body, and being judged for how one's body looks as it moves through the air.

12. When were the first eating disorder cases documented?

Eating disorders were rarely discussed prior to the 1970s. Hilde Bruch published a groundbreaking book in 1973 entitled *Eating Disorders: Obesity, Anorexia Nervosa, and the Person Within*. Bruch detailed 70 case studies and argued that eating disorders were more widespread than originally thought.

Prior to the 20th century, there was historical evidence of anorexia nervosa and other disordered eating behaviors. For example, in 700 BC, binge and purge episodes were reported among the Romans during the time of Caesar. The wealthy Romans would gorge themselves on extravagant banquets until they were overfull. Then, they would purportedly purge by vomiting to continue feasting. Disordered eating behavior was revealed in ancient Egyptian hieroglyphics depicting monthly purges to prevent illness. There are additional examples of African tribes who engaged in fasting and restricting behaviors to the point of having fatality risk, even after famines ended.

Religious fasting and showing hatred for one's body was also evident in women in the Christian era. In the 12th and 13th centuries there were examples of eating disorders tied to religious figures such as the Saint Catherine of Siena. She was said to have refused food to demonstrate her devout religious commitment and a denial of self. Early cases of eating disorders in the 17th century were referred to as the *wasting disease* to highlight the fasting behavior and marked weight loss of people. One such case of anorexia nervosa was described as occurring in England during the 1680s. A 20-year-old woman who was diagnosed with anorexia nervosa and died from her illness was characterized in terms (e.g., having a skeleton-like appearance) that resembled today's description of anorexia nervosa.

Sir William Gull was a physician who brought attention to the complexity of anorexia nervosa. Gull realized that anorexia, as a disease, represented more than a religious or biological eating practice. In addition to recommending force-feeding his female anorexic patients, Gull recognized the contribution of mental state and discussed the need for a change of scenery. He referred to the disease as *anorexia hysterica* to underscore the mental health component of the disorder *anorexia nervosa*, which literally meant *loss of appetite*. A French psychiatrist, Charles Lasegue, discussed the contribution of family environment around meals to creating stress and anorexia nervosa in children who refused food as a rebellion. He also argued women who were suffocated and stressed in a relationship may refuse food.

Bulimia nervosa was less discussed in the medical community than anorexia nervosa. A case of a female patient struggling from bulimia was first identified in a medical context in 1903 by Pierre Janet. The patient was reported to secretly engage in binge episodes.

Interestingly, by the early 20th century anorexia nervosa was attributed to having an endocrine problem. Thus, clients with eating disorders in the early 1900s were treated with pituitary hormones. There was also speculation on the part of physicians that anorexia nervosa was a form of tuberculosis. In the 1930s, an emotional connection was identified to the disease to shift thinking in the medical community. Cases described during this time underscored the obsessive nature around food and a drive for thinness by patients, leading to eating disorders and suicide. The multifaceted nature of this disorder was an important step in understanding an illness that remained very much a mystery.

A physiological and psychological connection to the disease was emphasized when anorexia nervosa was included in the first *DSM* in 1952, In the second edition (*DSM-II*) anorexia was listed under special symptoms in the feeding disturbances section; however, bulimia nervosa and binge eating disorder were absent from the manual. It was not until 1980 that bulimia nervosa was included as a mental health disorder in the newly designated eating disorders section in *DSM-III*. Although the clinical criteria for binge eating disorder were included in the appendix of *DSM-IV*, it was not until the recent edition of the *DSM-5* (2013) that binge eating disorder was included as a separate category in the eating disorders section.

By the 1970s and 1980s, both anorexia nervosa and bulimia nervosa were widely documented in the medical community but less understood by the general public. Early cases were thought to primarily afflict upper-class females. Well-known musician and singer Karen Carpenter brought widespread attention to the severity when she died in 1983 from heart failure associated with her long-term anorexia nervosa. The first free-standing eating disorder treatment center in the United States, Renfrew Center, opened in 1984 in Philadelphia.

13. What is "exercise bulimia" or "exercise addiction"? How many people suffer from this condition?

Exercise is generally considered a healthy behavior. Exercise has been shown to positively affect cardiovascular fitness, flexibility, bone health, muscular strength, and endurance and reduce body composition or body fat percentage. Given numerous benefits, exercise has been shown to reduce risk for cardiovascular disease, cancers, diabetes, and over-weight and obesity. In addition to physical benefits, exercise improves mental health by managing stress, by reducing depression and anxiety, and by elevating mood. Therefore, given the advantages associated with regular exercise, Americans of all ages are encouraged to be active. The recommended level of physical activity for adults is 150 minutes of moderate exercise per week or 75 minutes of vigorous or intense exercise weekly.

However, exercising too much, or obsessively exercising, can be damaging. Exercise can become a double-edged sword when injuries result from overexercise, or when exercise becomes an obligation that demands to be met. Health-related consequences for overexercise include overuse injuries, stress fractures, pressure sores, anxiety, fatigue, depression, mood swings, sleep disturbances, poor concentration, and irritability. Other negative effects include job loss, tension in social relationships, or poor academic performance.

Several terms have been used to describe an unhealthy relationship with exercise. Initially sport and exercise were viewed as solely positive by the general population. In the 1980s, *runner's high* characterized the euphoric rush after running long distances. The terms *exercise dependence* and *exercise addiction* that immediately followed were used to resemble both the highs and the lows. *Exercise addiction* refers to the addictive quality of unhealthy exercise, when intense workouts cause brief moments of euphoria. Once exercise stops, an individual will experience exercise withdrawal similar to what is associated with substance abuse. Also, individuals with exercise addiction will report increased *exercise tolerance*—requiring harder or longer workouts to get the same level of satisfaction.

Other terms used to represent the dysfunctional relationship with exercise include *compulsive exercise, excessive exercise, obligatory exercise, overexercise,* and *dysfunctional exercise. Exercise bulimia* has been used in the popular press to characterize using exercise to purge food. Clinicians in the eating disorder field prefer the term *dysfunctional exercise* to express the need for a client to change his or her relationship with physical activity. Both the amount of exercise and mind-set around exercise should be addressed.

Signs and symptoms of dysfunctional exercise include (1) following a rigid routine with narrow types of physical activity counting as exercise; (2) compelled to exercise even when one is sick, tired, or injured; (3) obligated to exercise when on vacation, stressed, and when unable to exercise; (4) prioritizing an intensive exercise regimen above family, work, and school; (5) increasingly socially isolated and spending more time alone; (6) not allowing rest days without experiencing intense guilt; and (7) experiencing exercise tolerance where more exercise is needed to calm down. *Primary exercise dependence* refers to having problems with overexercise and no eating disorder identified. By contrast, *secondary exercise dependence* is defined as an eating disorder (anorexia nervosa, bulimia nervosa, or binge eating disorder) as the primary diagnosis with the presence of unhealthy exercise behavior as a purging method.

The prevalence of exercise addiction and exercise bulimia is difficult to estimate; however, certain groups appear to be more at risk. It has been predicted that 33 to 78 percent of individuals with eating disorder suffer from a dysfunctional relationship with exercise. It is noteworthy that excessive exercise at the time of discharge for eating disorder treatment has been one of the strongest predictors of relapse. Therefore, it is important to treat an individual's mind-set surrounding exercise as part of a comprehensive therapeutic approach.

---❖---

Contributing Factors for Eating Disorders

14. What causes eating disorders?

One of the most common questions to be asked about eating disorders is what causes them. Although eating disorders can be present among people of any age, sex, race, ethnicity, or income bracket, there are several contributing factors that have been identified to predispose a person to eating disorders. These contributing factors are often referred to as *causes*; however, there is generally not a single cause when a person develops an eating disorder. Instead, it should be emphasized that multiple contributing factors come together to increase the likelihood that someone will develop an eating disorder. Another important caveat to mention is that not everyone who has certain vulnerabilities or has been exposed to contributing factors for eating disorders will develop disordered eating behaviors. As noted previously, it is critical to remember that eating disorders are a complex mental health disorder. Some of the vulnerabilities or risk factors can include but are not limited to mental health concerns, social and environmental triggers and pressures, influences in a family, or genetics. These frequently analyzed "causes" of eating disorders will be discussed here.

Mental Health Concerns

It is important to note the role of psychology in the development of an eating disorder. Is there a common personality type among people who have eating disorders? Probably not, but researchers have found that individuals more likely to develop eating disorders have several common psychological characteristics. Some of these psychological tendencies include possessing high expectations for self, perfectionism, a sense of inadequacy, low self-esteem, hypersensitivity to criticism, and difficulty identifying and expressing emotions. Another common psychological feature or comorbidity discovered among individuals with eating disorders is the tendency to also present with a mood disorder (e.g., depression), anxiety disorder, or obsessive-compulsive disorder. Finally, clinicians have recently reported that individuals with eating disorders commonly exhibit a similar propensity to avoid conflict and risk.

Having high expectations for oneself is not necessarily a bad thing. Striving for big goals can result in achieving success and can be a positive characteristic. In fact, individuals with eating disorders who have a tendency to be achievement-oriented have often been "A" students who excel in academics, sports, and other activities they pursue. This driven personality can lead to working hard to meet goals. However, many individuals with eating disorders exhibit perfectionism—that is, the tendency to try to be "perfect" or do things 100 percent all of the time. Perfectionism reinforces high expectations and can result in success unless perfectionistic tendencies lead to second-guessing or stalling behavior that can reinforce perfectionism, the characteristic to have extremely high expectations for self. This tendency is pervasive in individuals with anorexia nervosa and may be viewed as a positive way by others who perceive perfectionistic tendencies as a sign of a disciplined person.

Having low self-esteem and a sense of inadequacy is also common in individuals with eating disorders. Eating disorders are a way to cope and reflect a belief of never being good enough (e.g., thin enough, pretty enough, smart enough). Some people with eating disorders hope that when they lose a certain number of pounds, they will suddenly be happy or more confident. Unfortunately, the cycle usually spirals out of control with too much weight lost and even worse perceptions of self. An eating disorder can be a deeply entrenched part of a person's identity if he or she associates thinness with success or popularity.

Another common risk factor for eating disorders is hypersensitivity to criticism. Although all of us receive negative comments on occasion, individuals at risk for developing eating disorders are especially sensitive to the social environment and the emotions of those around them. Comments have a more intense and amplified effect on one's psyche. There is difficulty letting go of negative comments that are remembered for years. Studies have consistently found that individuals who have been teased for their weight or who are developing sexual characteristics (e.g., puberty) are at risk for an eating disorder.

Having an existing mental health disorder is another risk factor for developing eating disorders. Depression and anxiety are both correlated with disordered eating and eating disorders. Another common coexisting disorder is obsessive-compulsive disorder, characterized by patterns of obsessive behaviors. Recently, researchers at University of Virginia found a link between bulimia nervosa and attention-deficit/hyperactivity disorder. An explanation for this link is the shared characteristic of impulsivity.

The inability to identify or express appropriate emotions is a common psychological feature and risk factor for eating disorders. In some cases, a person may lack a healthy outlet to express anger or other intense emotions. An eating disorder can be the way to cope, rather than confront a situation. The tendency to avoid expressing emotions has been associated with increased risk for disordered eating.

In recent years, clinicians have noted the common tendency of individuals with eating disorders to avoid stress, conflict, or strife in their relationships and life. For example, a frequent way this avoidant personality plays out is that clients are risk-averse across situations. This can apply to something like jumping out of an airplane but relates strongly to taking emotional risks. Having emotional vulnerability creates anxiety among individuals with eating disorders. Therefore, in an effort to avoid feelings of anxiousness, individuals with eating disorders avoid conflicts in interpersonal relationships or any expression of strong emotions. This avoidant behavior can lead to problems with communication in one's interpersonal relationships.

Social Environmental Triggers and Pressures

In addition to psychological characteristics, there are numerous social factors that increase the risk of an eating disorder. Exposure to media messages and unhealthy ideals has shown to increase body dissatisfaction. Socially constructed body ideals are very thin for women and hypermuscular for men, both unattainable physiques. Images are hypersexualized and are associated with the message that to be successful one must look a particular way.

Specific social environments may be particularly ripe for the development of an eating disorder. For example, an athletic environment has been found to have numerous pressures related to body weight, shape, and size. Athletes may be expected to weigh a particular amount (e.g., jockeys) or a particular weight class (e.g., boxers) to compete. The perception that if weight changes, performance will improve can also drive unhealthy weight control methods. Aesthetic sports, such as figure skating, diving, and cheerleading, may involve wearing revealing costumes or uniforms that draw attention to the body and one's perceived flaws. Comments by coaches, judges, and other athletes may also contribute to negative consciousness of one's appearance. Similarly, other performance contexts may also influence eating disorders. Dancers need to be a particular size to progress to professional ranks and be selected by a choreographer. Dancers, actresses, and other performers face intense scrutiny over what they wear and how they look.

Other social groups that emphasize cohesiveness and unity may also present risk for the development of an eating disorder. Sororities may intensify the pressure to conform by looking a particular way and focus on appearance. Additionally, these groups of similar-aged women can encourage dieting or disordered eating behaviors through the sharing of unhealthy eating fads that may include fasting, restricting certain foods, unhealthy cleanses, and purging through vomiting, the use of laxatives, and excessive exercise. These peer groups may also perpetuate a culture that emphasizes fat shaming or that being large is negative. The likelihood of body-related comments, direct or indirect, has also increased in these groups of women.

Family Influences

In the past, a family dynamic of an overprotective mother and a distant father was blamed almost exclusively for the negative eating patterns of girls and young women who had no genetic or other environmental risks. Although that early view of eating disorders is overly narrow, the influence of dysfunctional relationships and poor communication persists. Families thought to have difficulty with emotional expression may cultivate environments that encourage eating disorders. Another potential risk factor is the presence of extreme pressure to perform in academics, sports, or social settings. This achievement-oriented family culture coupled with genetics and personality characteristics has contributed to the tendency toward disordered eating.

Parents and siblings serve as role models of both positive and negative forms of eating behavior and dieting. Weight-related comments by family members can have a detrimental effect on one's body image and eating behaviors. For example, a mother who criticizes her body is displaying both the importance of appearance and body dissatisfaction.

Genetic and Biological Factors

More attention has been given to genetic factors that represent an important contributing factor for eating disorders. Researchers have linked genes to cases of anorexia nervosa in Swedish twins. A separate study, the Minnesota Twin Study, found genetic effects related to the development of eating disorders in girls aged 14–18. An individual with a mother or sister who has an eating disorder is 4 times more likely to develop bulimia nervosa and 12 times more likely to develop anorexia nervosa. Similar studies have replicated findings that relatives with anorexia and bulimia nervosa were more likely to develop eating disorders than someone with no family history of eating disorders. Heredity is also an important contributing factor for binge eating and obesity.

Brain chemistry has also been suspected in the development of eating disorder. Serotonin and neuroepinephrine are norepinephrine that provide a sense of emotional and physical satisfaction. Specifically, serotonin lets us know when we are full and have eaten enough. Interestingly, initial studies have discovered that individuals with eating disorders and depression have lower levels of serotonin and neuroepinephrine than individuals who do not suffer from these mental health disorders.

Additionally, individuals with eating disorders exhibit higher levels of cortisol than people who do not suffer from disordered eating. Cortisol is a hormone released in times of stress. People with eating disorders have also tested at higher levels for neuropeptide and peptide. Elevated neuropeptide and peptide levels have been demonstrated to increase food consumption in animal studies. Finally, another hormone, cholecystokinin (CCK), has been found to create a sense of satiation. However, individuals with bulimia nervosa were found to have low CCK levels, which would correspond with an inability to identify a sense of fullness after eating.

15. What do academics have to do with eating disorders?

Academics, like sports and other performance contexts, can be ripe for the development of disordered eating behaviors and eating disorders.

Academic environments are highly charged with assessment tools that benchmark a student's progress and success against his or her classmates. Ultimately, how a student performs in an academic setting can influence the student's success in life, what college he or she gets accepted into, and what job he or she can hold in the future. Therefore, most parents are deeply committed to the academic achievement of their sons and daughters. Parents can add pressure by making comments about the importance of exceling in classroom and in grades. Teachers can make comments that demonstrate the way students are being successful or failing to achieve at a necessary level.

Students who are particularly sensitive to stressful environments, being compared to others, and experiencing pressure to be perfect may be particularly vulnerable to using unhealthy methods for coping. Typically coping involves using a behavior that is within a person's control in an attempt to feel like a chaotic situation is being managed. Restricting one's eating or limiting certain types of food can be one dysfunctional coping mechanism. Unfortunately, this "stress management strategy" can start off innocently enough before spiraling out of control. Pretty soon, an individual can feel compelled to persist in the disordered eating behaviors, and they may be used to regulate one's emotions.

Academics are especially likely to breed eating disorders due to the focus on strong achievement and being perfect. Both perfectionism and achievement-orientated characteristics are common among individuals with eating disorders who also tend to have low self-esteem. A student who wants to be the "top" student or earn all A's may feel the need to do whatever it takes (e.g., staying up long hours studying) to be successful even if it is detrimental to the student's health.

Individuals who experience pressure to be successful in academic realms may use a wide variety of disordered eating behaviors and can fit the criteria for clinical eating disorders, including anorexia nervosa, bulimia nervosa, and binge eating disorder. It is important for the comprehensive treatment plan to address how academic stressors will be managed moving forward in recovery to eliminate dysfunctional coping strategies.

16. What does age have to do with eating disorders?

Eating disorders affect people of all ages. Although there has been a prevailing myth (see misconception in the "Common Misconceptions about Eating Disorders" section at the beginning of this book) that people can outgrow negative body image and eating disorders, the belief that people magically stop having body dissatisfaction and disordered eating is flawed. Young women and men who are in their adolescent years from early teens and into college are at increased risk for developing eating disorders for a number of reasons. First, as individuals grow into their teenage years, there is a heightened focus on the meaning of appearance within peer groups and the opposite sex. Ideals about how one should look are reinforced in many ways, such as advertisements in the media. Seeing so-called perfect physiques in magazines and online can contribute to negative feelings about one's body. Comments from peers and family members can play a role as well. However, these internalized feelings about one's body and the importance of how one appears to others never really goes away.

One study that surveyed women from 20 to 80 years of age found that they were dissatisfied with their bodies regardless of age. In fact, the group that exhibited the highest body dissatisfaction scores had women between 40 and 60 years of age. Body dissatisfaction is an important indicator as it is the strongest predictor of eating disorders. These middle-aged women attributed their negative body image to feeling "out of their prime" and age-related bodily changes. Some of the notable responses were related to facial lines and wrinkles, increased body mass and cellulite, and graying hair. Women seemed to believe that they needed to preserve their youth at all costs whether engaging in costly plastic surgery or buying expensive anti-aging creams. Men, on the other hand, were seen as distinguished, which was not necessarily viewed in a negative way.

Certain life milestones have been attributed to the increased risk for eating disorders. For example, pregnancy has been demonstrated to influence eating behaviors in a positive or negative direction. Some women improved their nutritional habits with an eye to the baby on the way with the idea of eating for a benefit greater than self. However, other women fought the inevitable weight gain associated with pregnancy. These women continued to exercise and in some cases dangerously restricted food intake. After having the baby was another period of time that was representative of disordered eating behaviors. "Losing the baby weight" has been highly illustrated in magazines as celebrity pre- and post-delivery photos demonstrate a quick return to original shape post-pregnancy. Excessive exercise and dieting were common among women after they had a baby.

Another noteworthy milestone was menopause. Women found that their bodies would tend to store fat in undesirable places. This physiologically driven bodily change has not been well received. Therefore, post-menopausal women were also at risk for developing eating disorders and having a negative body image. Ultimately, a person of any age could experience body dissatisfaction and develop or continue his or her eating disorder.

17. What role does genetics play in the development of eating disorders?

Much emphasis has been placed on the role of the media in triggering eating disorders; however, genetics have been recognized as an important factor for one's predisposition for developing certain mental health disorders. In fact, the metaphor has often been used that genes act to "load the gun" when it comes to eating disorder risk, while environmental factors such as television advertisements, family role models, and peers can serve to "pull the trigger" for an eating disorder. There are continuous debates about whether genetics or sociocultural factors more strongly contribute to the development of disordered eating. In reality, it is challenging to separate out the biological factors or genetics (also referred to as *nature*) from the environmental factors (also referred to as *nurture*) when looking at the influences one's family may play on the development of disordered eating. It has been estimated that 28 to 83 percent can be tied to genetics for bulimia nervosa whereas approximately 58 to 88 percent was associated with genes for anorexia nervosa. These numbers represent large ranges, which make it difficult to pinpoint the direct role that genetics may play in a person's susceptibility for later disease development.

Twins provide useful information when studying the contribution of genes for disease development. In fact, a key indicator that confirms a genetic connection to mental health concerns is found by examining the presence of eating disorders in identical versus nonidentical twins. When comparing identical twins, who share biology and have identical gene composition, to nonidentical twins, the differences in eating disorder incidence across both twins are staggering. Only 5 percent of the nonidentical twins both developed eating disorders. However, twins were much more likely to both develop eating disorders—56 percent of both twins reported having eating disorders. Stated another way, it is estimated that a female identical twin will be 10 times more likely to develop the disorder if her twin suffered from the problem. When considering the relationship between genetics and the development of bulimia nervosa and binge eating disorder, the association is much less clear and more research is needed to make definitive predictions.

Examining genetic links with mental health disorders that represent common comorbidities can be another way to indirectly study the biological connection to develop eating disorder later. For example, the presence of substance use disorders or alcohol abuse in biological relatives has been attributed to an addictive personality and may also contribute tendencies to binge eat. Finally, a history of depression in one's family has been tied to eating disorders due to the frequent comorbidity (i.e., co-occurrence) of the two disorders. The correlation with other family members including parents can be complex to measure. Although there is a clear genetic link in these cases, there are also environmental factors to consider such as the role modeling effect. It is important to be mindful when addressing eating disorders that contributing factors or "causes" do not occur in a neat and organized fashion that allows for the study of individual factors. This combination of factors that may occur simultaneously makes the identification of the strongest causes and the necessary treatment approaches difficult to identify. Although one's genetic makeup may represent protection against eating disorders for certain individuals, they can still expect to face many pressures in society that can lead to a focus on body weight, shape, size, and appearance.

18. What role does the media play in the development of eating disorders?

Media is an easy target when it comes to identifying a tangible way that certain physiques are celebrated for men and women. When considering ideal body types for women, combing various forms of media allows one to determine that thin and feminine is desirable. For men, a body image of a masculine physique that is complete with a "six pack" of visible muscles is found readily online, in television ads, and in glossy magazines. A book by Naomi Wolf, entitled *Beauty Myth*, was published in the early 1990s, which illuminated the powerful relationship between media messages and body image for women. Specifically, Wolf suggested that advertisements teach girls and women to be dissatisfied with aspects of their appearance and to shoot for a better one. Luckily, commercials also provide the beauty-fixing "solution" in the form of an actual product to address those problem areas. If television or online ads portray models with perfect skin free of blemishes, moles, or bumps, men and women have images that represent what to strive for in their plight for beautification.

Like skin products, the media also teaches girls and men to be dissatisfied with the weight, shape, and size of their body or individual body parts. Media images represent models who have unique genetics (e.g., naturally very tall or slim) that have been airbrushed or photoshopped to perfection. Even if the consumer knows that images are altered, studies have found that messages are internalized as dissatisfaction. This dissatisfaction can be coupled with an increased vulnerability to take action. Commercials may advertise the latest diet product or weight loss plan in the interest of making money. Once the consumer is hooked, he or she will open the wallet. The diet industry represents big business. Media is merely the tool for getting consumer goods into the wider market.

19. What role does dieting play in the development of eating disorders?

People in the United States have an obsession with food. Historically food was a matter of survival and continues to be for people who face food security issues, wondering where the next meal will come from. However, some individuals in today's world are living with an overabundance of food choices. This excess contributes to a tendency toward both becoming overweight and obese, and having the privilege to go on a diet. A *diet* refers to restricting the amount or type of food one eats usually with the intent to lose weight or change one's body. In North America and across the world, there are numerous fad diets, such as the paleo diet, ketogenic diet, and South Beach diet. Furthermore, the weight loss industry is enormous and supports this dieting mentality that is so pervasive in our culture.

Paradoxically, most diets are found to be ineffective in helping individuals with sustained weight loss. Diets, like eating disorders, have also been associated with negative consequences such as experiencing feelings of guilt and increased depression. Mood swings are a common occurrence among individuals who are on a diet. Even more disappointing is that chronic dieters find that they often regain weight over a period of years. Depriving oneself of food can also undermine one's ability to gauge when he or she is genuinely hungry. This goes counter to a healthy eating philosophy of intuitive eating. Intuitive eating encourages individuals to move away from emotional eating and eat when they experience physiological cues of hunger. This approach also dissuades individuals from using a diet mentality, instead promoting a diet represented by diverse types of foods. Having no "good" or "bad" foods allows us to relinquish the power that food has over someone who is on a diet.

What is the real problem with dieting? Interestingly, having a mentality of restriction can feed one's tendency toward disordered eating. Although dieting is not always the only cause of eating disorders, it can contribute to a dysfunctional mindset around food and our bodies. In fact, many people begin a diet innocently to lose a few pounds. Unfortunately, this diet can lead to an obsession with calorie counting or restricting foods to get continued results. Alarmingly, to support this tendency the National Eating Disorders Association reports that 35 percent of "normal dieters" progress to pathological dieting and that 20–25 percent of those individuals develop eating disorders. It is far too common that eating disorders start off as dieting and can be considered a risk factor for increased likelihood (i.e., 5 to 18 times more likely) to present eating disorder behaviors. It is problematic that dieting has become common and normalized in our society. Dieting behavior starts young in our society as children aged 9 to 11 are found to engage in dieting at alarming rates. A study published in the *Journal of the American Dietetic Association* in 1992 found that 46 percent of 9 to 11 year olds are "sometimes" or "very often" on diets and that 82 percent of their families are "sometimes" or "very often" on diets. It would not be surprising if the rates have increased over the years, especially since that has been the trend of the dieting industry. The weight loss industry is worth around $61 billion, but it is clear that the methods used are rarely successful and often psychologically harmful.

20. What role do sports play in the development of eating disorders?

Sports can be a double-edged sword when it comes to eating disorders and body image. On the one hand, athletes may have certain protective factors due to sport participation that may lower their risk for eating disorders. For example, sports can foster positive values such as helping to build confidence, teamwork, and working toward goals that may not be directly related to appearance. In fact, sports may act as a buffer against developing a distorted body image and dysfunctional view of eating. Further, sports can underscore the importance of power and strength and may reinforce the notice of consuming "food for fuel." This healthy eating philosophy combats common notions of dieting and constantly wanting to lose weight.

On the flip side, however, sports can become a breeding ground for eating disorders if the importance of body weight, shape, and size is overemphasized within the athletic context. Athletes are often portrayed as both role models and possessing the ideal physique for a man or woman.

Athletes tend to share a similar psychological profile with eating disorder clients. That is, athletes are extremely goal-oriented, are high achievers, and strive for perfection. One noteworthy distinction is that athletes tend to report higher self-esteem than individuals with eating disorders. Therefore, it is athletes who are sensitive to criticism and have lower self-esteem that might be at risk for developing disordered eating behaviors in response to the pressure to change bodies for sport.

Although eating disorders may occur regardless of whether someone is playing a sport and at any age, there is evidence that certain sports carry a greater risk than others. Although athletes who play sports that do not seem to be associated with a particular "look" or body type may be lower at risk than even the general population for developing eating disorders. By contrast, so-called leanness-demand sports refer to sports that value a thin or lean body type and emphasize physical qualities in order to excel in sport. Athletes who compete in leanness-demand sports may be more vulnerable than non-athletes or athletes from nonleanness-demand sports for engaging in disordered eating behaviors, including food restriction, purging behaviors, and excessive exercise.

Prevalence studies have been inconsistent in findings as have been studies that compared the incidence of eating disorders between athletes and non-athletes. One exception was a Norwegian study that compared elite athletes to other athletes who were less competitive and non-athletes. Elite athletes were much more at risk for disordered eating than either of the other groups. Differences between athletes and non-athletes were more likely to be pronounced when athletes from leanness-demand sports such as distance running, gymnastics, or diving were included in the study. A recent U.S. study that surveyed collegiate athletes revealed that 19.2 percent of males and 25 percent of females could be classified as symptomatic for an eating disorder. Moreover, competitive level could play a role with respect to eating disorder risk. On the one hand, certain athletes who do not fit the desired body type for one's sport may get "weeded out" before they reach elite levels of participation. However, those athletes performing at elite levels may also be more willing to go to extremes to enhance their performance and gain an advantage over their opponents.

Interestingly, depending on the sport, athletes may be encouraged to lose weight or gain weight. Football players in certain positions, for example, may be pushed to eat more and put on the pounds with the rationale that they will be more competitive. Female cheerleaders, by contrast, may be expected to lose weight in order to try out for their sport and to execute stunts with partners. Boxers or wrestlers may be prompted to gain or lose weight to compete in a different weight class.

This perception that one needs to change one's weight, shape, size, or appearance for sport has been referred to as weight pressure. Sources of weight pressure may be the coach, other athletes on the team, self (i.e., internal), judges, parents, or other significant sport professionals (e.g., choreographers, athletic trainers, team doctors). Weight pressures can include weight limits or weigh-ins that build awareness about the number on the scale. Further, comments that relate to the importance of size or weight can create weight pressures for athletes. Athletes have reported that the team uniform, especially in cases wherein the attire is form-fitting and revealing, is one of the most common types of weight pressures in sport. Athletes from a variety of sports indicate that uniforms that are ill-fitting or that do not hide perceived bodily flaws can contribute to intense body dissatisfaction. Ultimately, understanding the presence of weight pressures among athletes is important for two reasons. First, weight pressures within the sport environment can represent a contributing factor for the development of an eating disorder or disordered eating behaviors. Second, from a competitive standpoint, athletes who are focused on how their body looks in a uniform may lose focus and concentration, and have decreased confidence to execute. This would likely inhibit their ability to perform at their optimal level, which should get coaches to pay attention.

21. What does religion have to do with eating disorders?

Like sports, religion can be a double-edged sword when it comes to healthy eating or disordered eating behaviors. On the one hand, religious practices that involve fasting as a symbol of one's conviction or faith can be dangerous reinforcements of anorexia nervosa. By contrast, spirituality or having something to believe in can be powerful when one is faced with adversity. Therefore, eating disorder treatment centers and providers have frequently incorporated spirituality into group therapy and the recovery programming.

Religion as a Contributing Factor or Reinforcement of Eating Disorder

When examining history, it is apparent that the early origins of eating disorders have some religious underpinnings. In the 12th and 13th centuries, women who fasted were held in high esteem and deemed to be saints. Fasting as a religious practice was seen as the ultimate way to demonstrate one's faith. This was particularly noteworthy for women who were often at risk for being labeled a "witch."

One example of such a saint was Catherine of Siena (1347–1380) who was regarded as Saintly within the church. Documentation of her story indicates that Catherine Benincasa's fasting behavior began at age 15. Her diet initially subsisted of uncooked vegetables, bread, and water and then grew gradually more restrictive. By 25 years of age, she refused to drink water and would spit out herbs after chewing them. Her life ended in her early 30s. For women, their bodies became the form of punishment and sacrifice in the religious context. These early practices of self-starvation and denial of food resemble anorexia nervosa as a disease but were not seen as pathological.

Fasting and self-starvation practices have continued throughout the centuries as a common thread across religions. Today fasting may still occur during certain periods of time (e.g., Lent) and is viewed as a religious practice. Unfortunately, having certain prescribed fasting periods can reinforce disordered eating, dieting, or food restriction.

Religion as a Positive Role in Treatment and Recovery for Eating Disorders

There is evidence that the practice of carrying out a healthy lifestyle in a variety of arenas (e.g., drinking alcohol, eating) is often revered and encouraged among certain religious groups. Therefore, mental health clinicians are careful to explore the meaning and perceptions of religion for each client. For some individuals religion and having faith represent a positive motivation to become healthy and recovered. Residential treatment facilities will frequently offer spirituality groups or Alcoholics Anonymous groups that emphasize having a higher power.

Although spirituality and one's faith can serve as inspiration to get better, other individuals who suffer from eating disorders find that religion can continue to offer a certain pressure (real or perceived) to continue engaging in restrictive eating practices. Therefore, it is important to avoid a "one-size-fits-all" approach for infusing spirituality into one's treatment plan.

22. What does a person's relationship with exercise have to do with eating disorders?

It is difficult to imagine how it is possible to get "too much of a good thing" when it comes to a healthy behavior like exercise. With obesity being referred to as a "global pandemic," eating healthy and exercise have been promoted extensively in the public. Michelle Obama's "Let's Move" campaign encouraged physical activity for entire families as part of an overall healthy lifestyle. The benefits of exercise are undeniable for both physical and mental health. The recommended amount of physical activity has been prescribed by the American College of Sports Medicine as 150 minutes per week for adults at a moderate intensity level or 75 minutes at a vigorous intensity. By engaging in regular exercise, children and adults can prevent overweight and obesity as well as diseases such as various cancers, diabetes, and cardiovascular problems. Physical activity helps promote bone health and can delay or prevent bone-related diseases such as osteoporosis. For all people, but especially aging adults, physical activity can assist with coordination, balance, and flexibility, which may prevent falls from occurring. From a psychological perspective, exercise has been shown to reduce depression, anxiety, and stress while improving overall mood and alertness. However, the importance of moderation is critical as exercise taken to the extreme can have negative effects on one's health.

Being physically active in an excessive amount or feeling compelled to exercise can be a characteristic of disordered eating. Dysfunctional exercise, which is defined as being both excessive in quantity and is characterized by feeling compelled to engage in a rigid routine, represents another compensatory method, similar to vomiting or using laxatives, and is associated with negative emotions and guilt. Having a negative relationship with exercise has been referred to as "exercise abuse," "exercise addiction," "compulsive exercise," or "exercise dependence" to demonstrate the parallel to other kinds of addictions and the negative aspects of an otherwise healthy behavior. A person who feels obligated to exercise may develop a tolerance to the amount of physical activity required over time in order to experience the feelings of euphoria or exercise-induced "high." Moreover, feelings similar to how withdrawal is described by addicts can emerge in the absence of exercise. Exercise dependence may occur with or without an eating disorder. When negative exercise behavior (i.e., excessive and compulsive) occurs in the presence of an eating disorder, it is considered to be secondary exercise dependence. Negative effects of exercise dependence can include physical and mental health consequences as well as implications for one's relationships.

Exercising excessively and to the extreme can contribute to pain, sickness, and injury. Other negative consequences include problems with sleep, irritability, and mood swings. Exercise is prioritized over other life responsibilities such as job and family relationships which can yield devastating results. Job loss, poor academic performance, and strained relationships have been reported to be correlated with having a dysfunctional relationship with exercise. Other psychological consequences include depressed mood, increased anxiety, decreased self-confidence and self-esteem, and loss of interest in eating or other activities. Importantly, physical activity no longer becomes enjoyable, which means the healthy aspect of exercise is gone.

It is estimated that 21 to 55 percent of individuals with eating disorders show signs of excessive and obligatory exercise behavior. Importantly, exercise is also associated with an early onset of the eating disorder, more symptoms of eating disorders, and longer persistence of eating disorder behaviors. Given that abusing exercise upon discharge is considered one of the strongest predictors of relapse for eating disorders, mental health providers must recognize the complexity of exercise when treating people with eating disorders. Ideally a person on the treatment team (e.g., dietitian or exercise specialist) serves in the role of assessing, monitoring, and processing feelings around exercise. In the past decade, programs that specialized in eating disorders have recognized the need to address exercise in treatment and recovery.

23. How does one's childhood and family exposure to eating behaviors have an effect on the later development of an eating disorder?

The actions of family members can be instrumental in developing one's thoughts, attitudes, and behaviors around food. These eating patterns can begin early in one's childhood and can impact one's philosophy around food as well as one's tendency toward later dieting behavior or the development of an eating disorder. One's parental figure can have a large impact on one's relationship with food; however, siblings and other close relatives may also play a role in the development of dysfunctional thoughts and behaviors.

Role Modeling Effect

One direct way that family members play a role in sculpting attitudes toward food is by showing strong reactions to foods. Likes and dislikes of certain foods may be conveyed, as well as value judgments about whether foods are "good" or "bad" to eat. For example, a mother who indicates out loud that she wants to "avoid carbohydrates" is sending a message that foods high in carbohydrates like pasta, potatoes, and bread must be bad and should be avoided. Likewise if a parent overeats or eats past the point of being full, binge eating is modeled as normative behavior. Parents and other family members can also model when to eat. For example, some mothers and fathers portray that it is important to eat when one's tank is empty (i.e., listen to physiological cues of hunger). By contrast, it is common for parents to demonstrate by their own behavior a tendency to eat in reaction to intense emotions (i.e., emotional eating). Researchers have concluded that emotional eating is a learned behavior. As babies we are born with the ability to intuitively eat when we are hungry and stop when we are satiated.

Dieting behaviors can be learned from parents as well as siblings and other relatives. If a family member restricts certain foods or is obsessive in watching calories, this behavior could contribute to the development of thinking that one should watch one's intake or be weight conscious. Ideally, parents and other family members can model that having a varied diet is more important than avoiding certain types of food.

Food as Reward

Parents have the best intentions when trying to get children to "eat their dinner" and "finish their plates." Unfortunately the common strategy for accomplishing a clean plate is to say to kids, "you can get dessert if you eat your vegetables first." This approach disregards an intuitive approach to eating that reinforces hunger and fullness as the guide of when to eat. Further, certain foods are seen as a higher value than others (i.e., reward). Naturally kids will seek out these "forbidden foods" or "rewards" as a result of this food hierarchy. Parents might also provide food as a reward for getting a good grade, having a strong performance in a piano recital, or trying hard on the baseball field. This teaches children that food is a benefit like a trophy. These types of rewards should be avoided to decrease the power of food.

Effects of Eating Disorders

24. What are the physical effects associated with an eating disorder?

There are numerous physical effects associated with eating disorders. Bottom line is that eating disorders affect all aspects of the body's ability to function. Many of these physical effects represent severe and long-term health consequences; however, some physical effects are short term and go away once disordered eating is eliminated. Anorexia nervosa may result in adverse consequences ranging from infertility to death; bulimia nervosa can cause electrolyte imbalances and heart failure.

Physical Complications of Anorexia Nervosa

Cardiovascular complications are a frequent consequence of anorexia nervosa. These complications include irregular heartbeats, heart attacks, and heart valve collapse. Unfortunately, health consequences related to heart problems are serious and can result in death. When an individual who suffers from an eating disorder dies, it is often attributable to cardiovascular complications.

In addition to the cardiovascular system, one's nervous system is adversely affected by anorexia nervosa. Persons who suffer from anorexia nervosa may experience detrimental cognitive effects in ability to learn new information and retain information. Memory is affected negatively by disordered eating behavior (i.e., restriction). Individuals with anorexia nervosa often report having an inability to concentrate on the task at hand, which can have a negative impact on their school and work performance.

One of the areas of concerns for individuals with anorexia nervosa is the potential to negatively impact their ability to reproduce. Infertility, another negative effect of anorexia nervosa, is a serious health consequence. It is estimated that only half the individuals diagnosed with anorexia nervosa reestablish a menstrual cycle or return to normal body weight. At one fertility clinic, researchers found approximately 20 percent of the women had an eating disorder or a history of an eating disorder. Women who are anorexic and become pregnant risk having premature babies and/or babies who have low birth weight. In one study, mothers with a history of anorexia nervosa were twice as likely to experience premature births, and their babies were six times more likely to die. Babies were less healthy and more at risk for jaundice and respiratory distress. Developmentally, these children were at increased risk for stunted growth, poor nutrition, and social/emotional problems.

Anorexia nervosa is also associated with poor bone and skeletal health. Adolescents who are anorexic may stunt their still-developing bones, putting them at an increased risk for osteopenia and osteoporosis later in life. Women who are already at increased risk for these conditions may be seen hunched over due to these diseases, which cannot be reversed. Related to bones is dental health. Tooth erosion is also common in individuals with anorexia, particularly when vomiting behavior is present. The dental office may be the first sign of detection given that this effect is fairly prominent and easily recognizable.

Physical Complications for Bulimia Nervosa

Many of the physical complications of bulimia mirror the complications seen in anorexia nervosa. For example, cardiovascular conditions, such as heart palpitations, irregular or missed heartbeats, hypotension, and heart failure, also occur in individuals who are bulimic. Frequent physical complications of bulimia nervosa involve the body's digestive system. Gastrointestinal problems seen in these individuals are constipation, diarrhea, dyspepsia, pancreatitis, and sore throats. Due to the vomiting behavior used to purge, individuals with bulimia nervosa may also exhibit skin irritation and develop calluses on the backs of their hands and fingers. Tooth decay and abscesses are often the result of acid erosion caused by frequent vomiting. Often, a dental office may be the initial point of detection of individuals with bulimia nervosa who present with dental complications.

Physical Complications for Binge Eating Disorder

Individuals with a binge eating disorder may exhibit some of the same physical complications as individuals with bulimia nervosa but not those associated with purging behavior (e.g., dental or skin problems). Additionally, problems, such as weight gain or obesity, may result from binge episodes and chronic dieting behavior. There are numerous known health consequences associated with obesity, including putting one at an increased risk for certain cancers, cardiovascular disease, and diabetes.

25. What are the effects on mental/emotional health associated with an eating disorder?

In addition to the physical effects detailed in the previous questions, eating disorders can result in negative psychological consequences. Starvation and diet abnormalities can affect the brain's plasticity, structure, function, and brain-to-gut communication. Individuals with eating disorders or disordered eating symptoms, including a restrictive diet, excessive exercise, or purging, may be at an increased risk for developing mood disorders. This can be explained by the biochemical response of depressive symptoms emerging as a result of low levels of Omega 3 and 6 fatty acids in the body. For persons with anorexia nervosa, brain structure and cognitive function are particularly affected. Cognitive inflexibility, manifested as decreased set-shifting ability, and attentional bias, in the form of weak central coherence, are often seen in these individuals.

Set-shifting refers to an executive function of the brain that allows a person to unconsciously change attention between tasks. People with eating disorders have problems with set-shifting in a range of tasks. As the brain receives less nutrition, there is a reduced flexibility and an inability to see the big picture or long-term. Additionally, there is a tendency for increased rigidity; ritualized, rule-bound behavior; tunnel vision; and rumination of thought. As this occurs, the obsession with weight and preoccupation with diet details, body shape, and eating control behaviors increases. Thus, a person's ability to perform cognitive tasks outside of thoughts around diet, exercise, and weight is diminished. This leads to emotional swings and other negative emotional symptoms seen in persons with eating disorders.

Some emotional symptoms that are observed in anorexia nervosa include irritable mood, social withdrawal, lack of emotional intelligence, an inability to understand the seriousness of a situation, fear of eating in public, and obsessions with food and exercise. For example, an individual with an eating disorder may experience intense mood swings with one moment showing elation and the next moment being morose. People with eating disorders may avoid other people entirely in an attempt to avoid the need for emotional expression or being discovered for their unhealthy mind-set around food. This social withdrawal is common and may be seen with clients declining social invitations from friends and family members. In addition, there may be a strong preference to eat alone so one can focus on discipline of food or performing particular rituals around food.

Food rituals refer to specific patterns of behaviors that are used repeatedly during meal time. These rituals, such as eating food in a particular order, are usually pathological, not based on any scientific fact, and are developed as an attempt to calm oneself down around food. Individuals with eating disorders may decide to eliminate certain foods or entire categories of food out of an intense fear of being gaining weight.

Emotional symptoms of bulimia nervosa and binge eating disorder include low self-esteem linked to body image, a sense of being out of control, guilt, embarrassment, shame, and withdrawal from friends and family. Similar to individuals with anorexia nervosa, there is a tendency to avoid being judged for others with respect to food consumed. For example, binge episodes may be met with comments that incite guilt from roommates or others like "how did you possibly eat all of that food in one setting?"

In all subtypes of eating disorders, there is a common emotional thread of sensations of worthlessness and isolation. Unfortunately, these negative emotions tend to reinforce the eating disorder behavior that is then in turn used as a negative coping strategy. Studies have shown that people with eating disorders present lower health-related quality of life compared to other mental health disorders, including severe depression. It has been found in recent years that patients with binge eating disorder tended to report the lowest levels of health-related quality of life of all the types of eating disorders.

26. What are the effects on relationships and social health associated with an eating disorder?

Family, school, and social connections are all negatively affected by an eating disorder. As an eating disorder comes to dominate people's lives, it can severely strain friendships and romantic relationships. Prolonged illness can deplete the patience and resources of family and peers causing them to interact less with a person with an eating disorder. The loss of social connections and interactions can lead to later vocational and social impairment. Further, an individual with an eating disorder can experience social isolation from peers and family members, and loneliness will likely ensue. The tendency to hide negative behaviors can lead to secrecy and furthers this social withdrawal and alienation from others. Persons with eating disorders or disordered eating may also live with an overwhelming sense of shame or guilt associated with binge episodes, and this too has adverse consequences on social health.

Research suggests that the longer a person suffers from anorexia nervosa without proper treatment, the more relationship and social engagement difficulties are experienced. These may manifest as lower emotional functioning that include a lack of positive facial expression (e.g., smiling, laughing) and a person's sense of self. Accurate reading of the intentions and emotions of others is necessary for effective social communication. People with anorexia nervosa have impairments in this domain. They often are unable to recognize facial emotions, correctly interpret emotional meaning from voice or body movements, display emotional expression, or mirror emotions.

Neurocognitive features associated with abnormalities in social functioning become more severe the longer a person has the disease: meaning the longer an individual suffers from malnutrition and a restrictive diet, the more the ability to interact with others or recognize others' attempts to interact is lost. The longer this continues, there is an increased inability to understand welcoming facial and social cues and inability to give off approachable facial cues; thus an environment of isolation is created and continually reinforced.

While people with bulimia nervosa have little or no impairment in facial emotion recognition and do not seem to have negative effects in the executive function or social function domains of their brains, likely due to the difference in meal composition, they do experience similar symptoms of isolation and social withdrawal.

27. Can someone die from an eating disorder?

Yes, people can and do die from eating disorders. Anorexia nervosa received nationwide attention and notoriety when pop singer Karen Carpenter, age 32, died in 1983 from a heart attack associated with a years-long battle against her disease. Women with anorexia nervosa have twice the risk of dying compared to women with other psychiatric diagnoses. Deaths secondary to anorexia nervosa result from cardiovascular sequelae, severe emaciation, infection, gastrointestinal complications, or suicide.

Mortality is the fatality rate associated with a particular disease. Alarmingly, eating disorders have the highest mortality rate for adolescents of any mental health disorder. According to the National Institute of Mental Health, women aged 15–24 diagnosed with anorexia nervosa are 12 times more likely to die young than peers who do not have an eating disorder. One explanation for this higher death rate is the incidence of suicidality by people with eating disorders. The suicide rate in this group is 75 percent higher than individuals without an eating disorder. Mortality rates across studies range from 3.3 to 18 percent, with more recent studies and longer years of follow-up associated with higher mortality rates. Mortality rates are also correlated with severity of symptoms, increased impulsivity, duration of treatment, and in-patient hospitalization.

Not only young people die from eating disorders. Surprisingly, a high incidence of mortality was found in older individuals with anorexia nervosa. In fact, more than 78 percent of deaths secondary to anorexia nervosa were in people over age 45.

The mortality rate for bulimia nervosa is lower than anorexia nervosa (about 1%–3%), even though it and binge eating disorder are more prevalent. This difference in mortality rates is likely attributable to the little research and small number of long-term studies around mortality rates of bulimia nervosa and binge eating disorder.

Unfortunately, the longer a person struggles with an eating disorder without seeking treatment, the likelier he or she is to experience premature death. This trend is startling given that fewer than 45 percent of individuals with eating disorders report receiving treatment. Another predictor of mortality is the length of time a person struggles with an eating disorder. The American Psychiatric Association has reported that individuals who have suffered from anorexia nervosa for at least five years face increased risk of dying prematurely. This relationship has been confirmed by a separate study that estimated death occurs in 4–10 percent of individuals with anorexia nervosa. However, for people who suffer from anorexia nervosa longer than 20 years, the mortality rate increases to 20 percent. It is promising, however, that for people who are treated for an eating disorder, the mortality rate drops to 3 percent.

Dying from an eating disorder can occur from a variety of causes. People with anorexia nervosa tend to have multiple health conditions (comorbidities) and a poorer overall health status that contribute to early death. Common causes of death, other than suicide, are cardiovascular disease, including sudden death from a heart attack, stroke, esophageal rupture, infections (e.g., pneumonia), and cancer.

28. Are there other conditions that commonly occur with an eating disorder?

Yes, it is relatively common for individuals with anorexia nervosa, bulimia nervosa, or binge eating disorder to exhibit comorbidities along with their eating disorder. The most common psychological or mental disorders found among individuals with eating disorders include mood disorders, anxiety disorders, and obsessive-compulsive disorder (OCD). Alarmingly, a study of more than 2,400 individuals hospitalized for an eating disorder found 97 percent had one or more comorbidities. Of the participants 94 percent had co-occurring mood disorders with the vast majority meeting the clinical criteria for major depression disorder. Over half (56%) met the clinical criteria to be diagnosed with an anxiety disorder. Approximately one-fifth or 20 percent had the characteristics of OCD.

Other comorbidities found in the study that reflect tendencies in the eating disorder population included the following: post-traumatic stress disorder (PTSD), substance use disorders and addictions, and self-harming behaviors. In fact, 22 percent of participants were diagnosed with PTSD, and another 22 percent had an alcohol or substance use disorder. Over one-third of eating disorder patients (37%) were found to engage in self-harm behaviors on a regular basis. Having co-occurring conditions makes treatment and recovery much more challenging. Therefore, understanding the relationship between eating disorder and other mental health conditions is critical. Some of the commonly co-occurring conditions include depression, anxiety, trauma, substance use disorders, and personality disorders.

Depression and Eating Disorders

Mood disorders such as depression are commonly diagnosed among individuals with all types of eating disorders. It is estimated that half to three-fourths of individuals who have eating disorders have experienced depression throughout their lifetimes. Experiencing mood swings, irritability, and negative mood states are frequent symptoms that accompany disordered eating. Therefore, it becomes tricky to determine whether depressive symptoms are an outgrowth of an eating disorder or a true co-occurring condition. Understanding a client's history of depression is important along with any known family history. Antidepressants are frequently prescribed to treat symptoms of eating disorders with varied success.

Anxiety and Eating Disorders

Like depression, anxiety disorders are common among individuals with eating disorders. About two-thirds of the individuals with eating disorders also meet the criteria for an anxiety disorder. In many cases tendencies toward anxiety may appear in childhood and prior to the development of one's eating disorder. Some individuals with eating disorders have associated their disordered eating behaviors to be a direct response to stress and feeling nervous in a variety of situations. For example, *social phobia*, which refers to a fear of being around other people or in social situations, is a commonly diagnosed anxiety disorder for individuals with eating disorders. Another common anxiety disorder for individuals with eating disorders is OCD. OCD involves being caught in a cycle of experiencing unwanted and obsessive thoughts and feeling compelled to engage in ritualistic behaviors (i.e., compulsions). In addition to OCD and social phobia, other anxiety disorders frequently exhibited among individuals with eating disorders include generalized anxiety disorder (i.e., experiencing a heightened sense of stress or anxiety most of the time and across situations) and specific phobias (e.g., fear of bugs).

Trauma and Eating Disorders

Having a history of abuse in one's childhood or adult life is common among individuals with eating disorders. Abuse can be physical (e.g., hitting), verbal, or sexual in nature. Individuals who experience a traumatic event that threatens their safety or makes them helpless (e.g., physical or sexual abuse, military combat, or a natural disaster) may suffer from post-traumatic stress disorder (PTSD), another anxiety disorder. There is a high co-occurrence of PTSD and eating disorders. Therefore, treatment may be dedicated to understanding the meaning that this traumatic event (or events) have played in the development of one's cognitive mind-set and disordered eating behaviors.

Substance Abuse and Eating Disorders

About half of all individuals with eating disorders struggle with a substance use disorder (SUD). Several studies in the adult literature have reported an association between SUDs and eating disorders, with substance abuse present in 12–18 percent of adults with anorexia nervosa and 30–70 percent of adults with bulimia nervosa. Alcohol abuse is an oft-cited comorbidity of people with an eating disorder, and cirrhosis of the liver is another cause of death. People with eating disorders also tend to be tobacco users, which has known adverse health complications.

Personality Disorders and Eating Disorders. Personality disorders represent a broad category of mental health disorders that show enduring and maladaptive thoughts and behaviors. Because these "personality" tendencies are so deeply embedded in an individual's sense of self, the negative patterns are difficult to change. Further, personality disorders are often blamed for interfering with treatment progress and success. There seems to be a strong overlap between eating disorders and the existence of personality disorders, especially among inpatient populations. There are a number of types of personality disorders. Some of the common personality disorders identified among individuals with eating disorders include dependent personality disorder, OCD, and borderline personality disorder. Dependent personality involves having a lack of confidence in one's ability to make decisions or function on an everyday basis without excessive reliance on others. People who are diagnosed with dependent personality disorder may be described as "clingy" or overly needy. Because individuals with eating disorders often lack a strong sense of identity, this type of personality disorder may be present.

Personality Disorders and Eating Disorders

Obsessive-compulsive personality disorder refers to a general pattern of behavior that involves excessive concern with control over one's environment, being perfect, keeping a sense of order, and rigid inflexibility. Studies that focused on individuals with anorexia nervosa estimate that 12–20 percent could also fit diagnostic criteria for obsessive-compulsive personality disorder; for persons with bulimia nervosa, 11 percent receive a diagnosis for obsessive-compulsive personality disorder. For all other eating disorders, 11 percent of individuals were estimated to have obsessive-compulsive personality disorder.

Borderline personality disorder (BPD) refers to a specific personality disorder that involves difficulty in regulating one's emotions. Individuals with BPD often experience interpersonal difficulties and struggle to maintain healthy relationships with others. Additionally, BPD is characterized by having a negative image of oneself and tendency to be impulsive in actions and behaviors. It is estimated that approximately 6 to 11 percent of individuals with eating disorders also meet the clinical criteria for BPD. This prevalence rate of BPD is actually higher than the general population (i.e., 2% to 4% of individuals are diagnosed with BPD in the general population). People with BPD have a greater prevalence of eating disorders, with one study reporting that 53.8 percent of patients with BPD also met the criteria for an eating disorder.

Research on anorexia nervosa estimates that 10–25 percent of sufferers meet the diagnostic criteria for borderline personality disorder. For bulimia nervosa, 28 percent meet the criteria for borderline personality disorder. For all other eating disorders, 12 percent of the individuals meet criteria for borderline personality disorder. Signs and symptoms of psychological disorders may emerge around the same time as an eating disorder. However, signs can also appear before or after the development of an eating disorder.

29. Are eating disorders ever mistaken for other types of medical problems?

It is not uncommon for a person who is suffering with an eating disorder to schedule an appointment with a physician for a medical complaint rather to seek help from a counselor for their mental health disorder. It is common for individuals with eating disorders to receive medical treatment for specific symptoms that are assumed to be acute (e.g., stomach aches or sore throat) without being adequately assessed for deeper psychological problems. Various medical problems can be the logical outgrowth of disordered eating behavior and may be addressed as the primary problem rather than a symptom of the larger mental health disorder (i.e., eating disorder).

Gastrointestinal problems, which are readily reported by individuals with eating disorders, may be assessed for and treated as an isolated illness resulting from a stomach flu, virus, or stress rather than recognized as a symptom of an overarching eating disorder. This is especially problematic since common complications of disordered eating behavior such as restriction, purging, and other dietary changes can lead to acid reflux, heartburn, indigestion, nausea, peptic ulcers, abdominal pain, bloating, bleeding, and an increase in belching and/or flatulence. Related to gastrointestinal difficulties, acid reflux disorder or esophageal reflux is common among individuals with eating disorders. Other medical complications that can mimic eating disorder symptoms and thereby risk being treated in isolation are as follows: dehydration and anemia, electrolyte imbalance, hyponatremia, sleep disturbances, mononucleosis, and chronic fatigue syndrome.

An individual who is suffering from an eating disorder may report experiencing a sense of feeling weak, which may be mistaken to be merely dehydrated. Dehydration is caused by the depletion or lack of intake of fluids, or by restriction of carbohydrates and fat. Dehydration can mimic symptoms of restriction and starvation associated with a fear of gaining weight or retaining fluids as well as the use of laxatives or vomiting. Similarly, anorexia nervosa can be mistaken for anemia that results from an iron deficiency. Anemia can also occur due to malnutrition, there can be a lack in production of red blood cells, leading to iron-deficient anemia. Symptoms associated with anemia include an increase in fatigue, shortness of breath, and heart palpitations. Another frequent culprit of symptoms relates to electrolyte imbalances. Although electrolyte deficiencies can be associated with heavy training regimens, purging can also cause severe and damaging electrolyte imbalances. Specifically, purging has been linked to a loss of essential minerals that ensure healthy function of bodily organs, teeth, joints, bones, and muscles. When potassium levels are too low, hospitalization may be necessary.

Similarly, an individual with an eating disorder may present with symptoms of hyponatremia. When people go on a diet or restrict foods, sometimes food intake will be replaced with excessive water consumption. This increased water intake, which is often referred to as "water loading" can lead to this condition (i.e., hyponatremia). Drinking too much water can create a lack of sodium in the blood, which can create an electrolyte imbalance but can also cause fluid buildup in the lungs, brain swelling, nausea, vomiting, confusion, and even death.

While sleep disturbances such as insomnia are frequently recognized side effects of eating disorders, they are also common among the general population. Presenting with sleep problems can result in clients receiving medications for their sleep disorder but missing the eating disorder diagnosis. Individuals with eating disorders are particularly at risk for developing problems falling asleep or remaining asleep due to lack of nutritional intake and low blood sugar.

Another medical concern that may be mistaken for eating disorders is mononucleosis (i.e., mono). This illness has been associated with feeling weak and fatigued and lasts for weeks or even months. Because both mono and eating disorders are both common among teens and young adults, it is not surprising that some eating disorders can be initially mistaken for this illness. Moreover, the common symptoms of mono may begin with a sore throat or feeling tired, which can mimic the effects of purging behavior among individuals with eating disorders. Thankfully, a blood test can confirm the diagnosis of mono, but there can be a resulting delay in correctly identifying the problem as an eating disorder.

A complicated syndrome called *chronic fatigue syndrome* is associated with symptoms that may be present for individuals with eating disorders including sleep problems, sore throat, headaches, fatigue, joint pain, loss of memory or concentration, and extreme exhaustion that is not relieved by restful sleep. The author of this book who suffered from an eating disorder as a teenager was mistakenly diagnosed with chronic fatigue syndrome in the 1980s when she tested negative for mononucleosis and other medical concerns. In reality, the nutritional deficiencies resulting from her inadequate vegetarian diet coupled with a caloric intake that was not sufficient to meet energy demands from overexercise behaviors resulted in physical effects that mirrored this syndrome.

Eating disorders are associated with negative physical, psychological, and social effects. Because certain side effects can be common among the general population and individuals may seek medical attention rather than counseling support, it is easy for an eating disorder to be overlooked.

Treatment of Eating Disorders

30. How are eating disorders treated?

Eating disorders are complex mental health conditions and require a multifaceted treatment approach. A comprehensive program should involve a multidisciplinary treatment team that at minimum includes a medical doctor, dietitian, and mental health counselor. Initially a client may present with symptoms to any of these treatment team members. In fact, a client may be seeking treatment for physical symptoms associated with disordered eating behaviors. Conversely, a client may be entering treatment to address other mental health symptoms such as anxiety or depression. The first step for eating disorder treatment is for healthcare professionals to conduct an extensive assessment. Clinicians will use the *Diagnostic Statistical Manual of Mental Disorders, Fifth Edition* as a guide for assessing specific eating disorder symptoms and determining whether an individual meets the full criteria for a clinical eating disorder. The current edition classifies eating disorders into the following categories: anorexia nervosa, bulimia nervosa, binge eating disorder, and feeding disorders like avoidant/restrictive food intake disorder. The full description of symptoms for each type of eating disorder can be found in question 2 in the "Identification of Eating Disorders" section of this book.

The assessment process for eating disorders most commonly occurs in the form of an in-person or phone interview. Sometimes this appointment is referred to as an *intake interview*, but most often this is the session used to identify how severe the case is and to determine the level of care required. Eating disorder treatment centers frequently offer an assessment session free of charge. At this session, a trained clinician asks specific questions such as those around the history and extent of disordered eating behaviors, any substance use, relationship problems, and mood. The clinician should also assess for the existence of suicidal thoughts and self-harming behaviors. Once the clinician has conducted an assessment and determined the appropriate level of care (i.e., how much supervision is required), he or she can provide recommendations and referral as needed to local treatment resources. It will be important for the treatment providers and family members to work closely with insurance companies to get approval.

Levels of Care

Medical doctors should play an important role in determining the appropriate level of care as related to medical vulnerability, available support systems, and the client's motivation level. Specifically, *level of care* refers to one's need for supervision in all areas of life. The options for levels of care within eating disorder treatment are as follows from most intensive to least intensive: inpatient, residential, partial hospitalization, intensive outpatient, and outpatient.

The inpatient level of care is most restrictive and is limited to clients who require highest level of supervision. Inpatient may be required in locations where residential is not available or in cases wherein insurance will not support residential level of care. In addition to being extremely low weight or at medical risk, clients who attempt suicide report a vivid plan for committing suicide, or who are actively self-harming may be admitted into an inpatient setting. A client who is severely compromised may require intensive medical attention in a setting that resembles a hospital or is a hospital. In fact, hospitalization may occur for a medical issue before a client is diagnosed with an eating disorder. For example, electrolyte disturbances or other health-related consequences of disordered eating behavior may mimic other medical problems and result in admission.

Some eating disorder treatment centers offer inpatient level of care as a floor or wing, but for geographical regions that do not have the advantage of specialty care, the local hospital will be the likely placement. For someone in an inpatient setting, the focus will be on stabilizing vital signs and restoring body weight without sending the body into shock. In order to restore weight in an effective manner, the medical team may need to use a feeding tube or medically provide nutrients to the compromised patient. Because patients in an inpatient setting are in starvation mode, they are unable to work through deep-seated psychological issues in this medically compromised state. Once they begin to restore their weight to a point in which vital signs are stabilized, they may be able to transition to residential level of care.

The most popular setting for eating disorder treatment facilities is represented by residential level of care. Once medical stabilization has been achieved and the client no longer requires inpatient level of care, residential treatment allows for clients to engage in an extensive and structured programming to address all facets of eating disorders. Because clients are monitored in an environment that is supervised by staff 24 hours a day and 7 days a week, they have the opportunity to take risks and work through emotional issues in a safe place. There is typically nursing staff available around the clock who can monitor medication and can alleviate concerns as they arise. In a residential setting, clients will likely have the opportunity to participate in individual therapy with a mental health counselor selected to serve as their primary therapist during their stay several days a week to address personal issues and factors contributing to their eating disorder and relapse. In addition to participating in individual sessions to focus on personalized treatment plans and issues, group therapy is offered in most residential eating disorder facilities.

In group therapy sessions, which are typically led by a variety of facilitators with different expertise areas, clients have the opportunity to interact with others, which offers a shared experience and social support. Group therapy may be focused on a myriad of topics including but not limited to body image, spirituality, nutrition education, and cognitive behavioral therapy. Group therapy sessions may encourage counseling in a group setting or may be psychoeducational in nature. These psychoeducation groups tend to be run similarly to a class in that a strict lecture plan may be followed. In addition to offering individual and group therapy, many residential facilities encourage family therapy. Family sessions with identified caregivers are usually required for adolescents younger than 18 years. Family therapy may be encouraged for adults who are working through issues with specific family members or in their romantic relationship. These sessions are designed to educate family members on how to best support their loved ones in recovery upon discharge.

Working through nutritional aspects of treatment is also important in a residential setting. Clients will meet regularly with a dietitian who is assigned to discuss meal planning. Typically one-on-one sessions will be coupled with psychoeducation classes and groups. One such group is focused on intuitive eating. Clients will learn about how they have become emotional eaters who respond to stressors rather than biological cues of hunger and fullness. Intuitive eating as a philosophy encourages clients to eat a variety of foods with no "good" or "bad" options. Clients listen to their bodies to gauge their level of hunger prior to a meal and their level of fullness at the completion of a meal.

A physician or psychiatrist typically meets with residential clients on a frequent basis to determine medication types and doses. This treatment team member will also monitor vital signs and body weight (which is also measured by residential staff) and provide necessary medical information to insurance companies to continue coverage. The physician will also provide medical clearance to the client to participate in activities such as physical activity.

In addition to offering a variety of therapeutic formats with various treatment providers, another unique feature of residential treatment in specialized eating disorder facilities is the opportunity for clients to participate in a variety of complementary and alternative therapeutic approaches. A client may be exposed to equine or pet-assisted therapy to work through emotional issues in a safe and symbolic fashion. Music and art therapies may offer an outlet for expressing emotions in a nonthreatening and cathartic way. If medically cleared, recreation therapists will bring clients on outings to explore ways to be vulnerable and take risks whether it be a ropes course or hiking expedition. Yoga, which can be beneficial for some clients with eating disorders, has been provided as part of the residential programming. Other types of exercise may be added in gradually depending on the program and philosophy of the treatment center. Renfrew Center of Philadelphia, as an example, started one of the first exercise education programs in attempts to help clients work through overexercise issues during treatment. Clients in that program are provided both psychoeducation about exercise and experiential ways to explore exercise mentality without threatening weight restoration goals or medical status. A residential setting offers the luxury of employing exposure therapy to provide triggers in a safe environment with therapeutic support.

Despite having many advantages, residential level of care may be insufficiently supported by insurance companies due to being prohibitively expensive (e.g., $1,000 or more per day). Therefore, some clients might participate in partial hospitalization or intensive outpatient programs instead. The transition from residential level of care to partial hospitalization or intensive outpatient is often quite challenging for clients with eating disorders and represents a high risk of relapse.

Partial hospitalization level of care offers an alternative to stepping back to traditional therapy model of 50 minutes per week. Although many of the same elements of residential care are retained, such as group therapy sessions, meal monitoring, and individual work with a multidisciplinary treatment team, clients go to their home after the program. Some treatment facilities have provided a hotel-like setting for clients to reside while they are completing partial hospitalization for this step-down in care. By continuing to participate in intensive programming during the day, clients can save money and begin to work through challenging feelings and triggers that arise at night when they are on their own. If clients become suicidal or relapse, there can be the opportunity to admit them back into residential level of care.

Intensive outpatient is a lower level of care that is more cost-effective than residential and inpatient options. Some eating disorder treatment centers, such as Chrysalis Center for Counseling and Eating Disorder Treatment, which is located in Wilmington, North Carolina, are exclusively intensive outpatient. That is, a residential level of care is not offered. In these programs, clients come in for a half-day program several days per week to participate in comprehensive activities. The program will likely include individual sessions with a primary mental health therapist as well as dietitian. Clients will have some limited medical monitoring by a physician or psychiatrist who can also address medication types and make adjustments to dosage as needed. Programs may include cooking classes, group therapy sessions, family therapy, and exercise classes. Intensive outpatient is distinguished from outpatient as there is a higher frequency and more structure than traditional therapy. Insurance companies tend to prefer intensive outpatient as it can be a cost-effective form of treatment as compared to residential level of care.

Multidisciplinary Treatment Approach

Regardless of the level of care that is indicated for an individual who is being treated for an eating disorder, a multidisciplinary treatment approach is optimal to address the complexity of the disorder. The role of the medical doctor will be to assess and manage vital signs that relate to medical consequences for eating disorder. For example, electrolytes may be out of balance and can put client in dangerous medical risk or client may suffer from other medical consequences as a result of disordered eating behavior. As needed, the physician may prescribe medication to treat the physical symptoms (e.g., gastrointestinal distress) or mental health concerns (e.g., antidepressants). If client requires hospitalization, the medical person on the team can make necessary referrals. If body weight needs to be restored (especially in anorexia nervosa cases), this will likely occur at the time of the doctor's appointment and may involve tube feeding.

Weight monitoring may take place at medical appointments; however, sometimes the dietitian will take on this role if nutrition sessions occur more regularly in an outpatient setting.

The dietitian of the multidisciplinary treatment team plays a critical role to support client's nutritional plan and monitoring. A food plan will be developed to align with goals of weight restoration and stabilization. In some cases, the client may require additional supplementation to get caloric needs met and will require education around how to meet food group needs. The dietitian typically provides education around healthy eating. A focus on diversifying the diet will be important as part of eating disorder treatment as many clients will present with extremely narrow and restrictive diets. The dietitian may also be responsible for monitoring exercise patterns. By understanding the level of a client's physical activity, adjustments can be made to nutritional intake to stay on track for weight restoration and stabilization goals. However, the recent trend is to have an exercise specialist as an additional member on the treatment team. The exercise specialist can assess for excessive and dysfunctional patterns of physical activity. Additionally, this member of the treatment team can help promote healthy and balanced forms of exercise (i.e., intuitive exercise).

Finally, the mental health counselor will provide support for emotional aspects of treatment and recovery. Treatment will likely involve varied formats. Individual therapy is common for exploring personal issues and contributing factors to one's eating disorder. Moreover, comorbidities may be addressed such as substance use disorders and trauma history. Family therapy will be important to engage social support structures outside of the treatment provider context. Treatment with family members may involve parents if adolescents or siblings can be brought into session as needed. For adults, it is common to engage significant other or spouse in couples' therapy to discuss communication patterns. Finally, group therapy is common to address common themes that emerge across clients with eating disorders. Group therapy may entail a focus on body image, interpersonal relationships, intuitive eating (i.e., learning about mind-set of eating that involves hunger and fullness), spirituality, or another topic.

31. What is the best way to refer someone who may have an eating disorder to treatment?

If someone is suspected to have an eating disorder, it is important to be very delicate in the handling of a potential confrontation about the problem. Although it is a challenging circumstance without a doubt, there are a few recommended strategies to ensure that the message is received in a productive manner. It is critically important to determine the best person to have the conversation. Someone with power such as a coach may not be as ideal as someone who has established trust over time such as an Aunt or family friend. That person should be skilled at showing compassion in a firm way that is clear about their concerns. Once the right person has been identified (e.g., close friend, parent, sibling), he or she should schedule a time to discuss concerns in a private setting away from distractions and other ears. Sometimes people assume that having a large group discuss concerns about perceived problem will be more powerful in illuminating the issue around eating. However, it is important to emphasize that the popularly televised interventions with large group confrontations have not been shown to be effective for reaching individuals with eating disorders. Unfortunately, this approach may backfire and result in putting the person with suspected eating disorder on the defensive. Such a grand gesture may also cause embarrassment and be received as public-shaming rather than a group who has gathered to support their friend and family member in getting help for his or her struggle.

Having the Conversation

Rather than following the aforementioned large and public group "intervention" approach, the individual who has an established trusting relationship should schedule a time to talk privately. During this conversation, the person who is expressing concerns should use "I" words to state specific observations in a caring manner. Using "you" statements will likely cause the person to feel on the defensive. For example, saying "you are not eating anything. You need to eat" might result in having a person who is struggling with eating concerns to be more secretive in their behaviors and more closed off in their emotions. Instead it is recommended that the concerned and trusted person start by expressing concern from their personal perspective. "I'm really concerned about you. It seems like you are sad and not yourself. I care about you and want to be here for you." Concerns should be expressed with a calm voice that is not overly emotional. Many individuals with eating disorders will turn the tables and begin caring for the person who is attempting to confront.

Once the person has stated concern and caring for the person exhibiting disordered eating behavior, it is helpful to offer some specific observations in changes in behavior or mood. It is important to anticipate that the recipient of this conversation will be guarded in their response. Denial is a common response when individuals are confronted for disordered eating behaviors. Another likely response is to downplay the extent of the problem or their ability to resume healthy patterns of eating. The person who is struggling from an eating disorder may say something like, "I've been stressed out lately, but I'm going to get back on track and back to normal soon. This is just temporary." Moreover, it is important to be mindful that any interference in one's eating disorder behavior can be seen as threatening. There is the possibility that after feeling "called out" the person with disordered eating behavior may be more secretive. Although it is tempting to not say anything for fear of harming the relationship, it is important to keep in mind that you are planting the seed for when that individual is ready to seek help. Most likely it will not be at that very moment, but showing your support can help to build trust with the person and show your understanding. The conversation does not need to turn into a debate. The person expressing concern should continue to stay calm and firm. This will not be the last opportunity to express concern, support their family member or friend, or to offer resources.

Knowing the Resources

Although it is unlikely that the individual you have confronted about an eating disorder will be immediately prepared to seek treatment for their illness, it is still important to be ready with local, regional, and state resources. One of the keys to helping a person who is suffering from an eating disorder is to be aware of treatment providers, eating disorder treatment centers, and understand the intake process. However, finding local providers can be more challenging. A first start may be the closest eating disorder facility as they often offer free assessments and direct referrals within the community. However given that some states have one or no treatment centers that focus on eating disorders, it may be necessary to consider the university counseling center if a college student or a local counseling practice.

As online resources continue to expand, there are some assessment and treatment options available regardless of one's home address. However, the EDReferral.com website (https://www.edreferral.com) is a good place to start to identify national and state eating disorder treatment centers. The website offers a "find a therapist" link with referral options by zip code. Another option is going to the National Eating Disorders Association (NEDA) website (https://www.nationaleatingdisorders.org), which offers an eating disorder hotline. In addition to EDReferral.com and NEDA, some important listings and referral opportunities can be found at the end of this book within the "Resources" section.

Sometimes the conversation will lead to immediate action. In that case, it is important to be armed with resources as mentioned earlier as well as the willingness to help make the call, book the appointment, or transport the individual to an assessment session. As the support person one should know that at this initial session, a trained therapist will ask a series of questions to assess the type and severity of the problem. Usually these questions will involve some specific items around types of eating patterns and history of disordered eating. The responses will be kept confidential, so it will be up to the individual to share or disclose what happened in that session. Following this assessment session, the clinician will typically offer some options for treatment referrals and may help to facilitate booking a counseling session. The actual treatment process will be gradual and should be viewed as a long-term investment. There will likely be ups and downs during the treatment and recovery journey, so having a strong support network will continue to be a critical piece.

32. What nutritional approaches should be used for people with eating disorders?

Nutrition is a vital aspect of treatment for people who struggle with eating disorders. Although the point has been made throughout this book that eating disorders are not all about food, it is still necessary to address one's dysfunctional relationship with eating. This may involve assessment of current patterns of eating, as well as implementation of new ways of interfacing with food. Sometimes in cases where a client has severely restricted as part of his or her eating disorder, there might be a need for weight gain to occur as part of the nutrition component of one's treatment process. It is important to have an expert in nutrition as a member of the multidisciplinary treatment team to address eating disorders.

Nutritional support and treatment are often integrated into health care performed by a variety of healthcare workers; however, a registered dietitian is specifically trained to provide evidence-based nutritional treatment among diverse populations, including nutrition therapy for mental health disorders. A registered dietitian serves in the role of conducting assessments around eating habits, determining the personalized nutrition plan, and implementing nutrition interventions based on recommended healthy eating guidelines. Further, a registered dietitian helps an individual with an eating disorder understand his or her relationship with food. This may involve helping to normalize certain eating behaviors and challenging others. A dietitian often works to support an eating disorder client through concerns associated with consuming food (usually more and different kinds of food) and gaining weight. Nutrition education is also an ongoing part of sessions in order to defy food myths and help client understand what is healthy behavior around eating.

A registered dietitian is clearly a key player on a comprehensive and multidisciplinary eating disorder treatment team. In order to be effective in working with clients who have eating disorders, it is imperative for the registered dietitian to have a full grasp of the biological, psychological, and sociocultural aspects of eating disorders. The registered dietitian will be collaborating with other treatment professionals, who typically include a psychologist and physician at minimum, to devise and implement a treatment plan.

The role of the registered dietitian is centered around several key objectives: (1) to resolve medical complications associated with poor nutritional intake and habits, (2) to educate clients about the benefits of eating behaviors as necessary for physiological function, (3) to work to decrease fears and anxieties associated with food, and (4) to challenge and confront as necessary client's misperceptions around food and weight. The first step is to conduct a comprehensive assessment around nutrition and exercise behaviors. Once deficiencies are determined, the registered dietitian can work with the client to identify appropriate goals around nutrition. Nutrition goals will likely involve education around what nutrients are necessary and may require meal planning (i.e., plotting certain amounts of food or types of food to be consumed throughout the day in order to meet diverse nutritional needs). Treating eating disorder clients also involves having the registered dietitian work in collaboration with the physician or medical representative on the treatment team to identify and monitor a healthy target weight range for the client based on his or her body type, height, and history of body weight. In order to monitor weight changes, registered dietitians will generally conduct frequent weight checks in which the client gets on a scale during his or her appointment.

In order to address exercise behaviors, it is ideal to add a separate person to the treatment team who is a trained exercise science expert who understands the eating disorder population. This person (e.g., exercise therapist, physical therapist, personal trainer) can help client to identify specific treatment goals related to exercise. Moreover, the exercise therapist can also discuss the role of psychology in exercise and how to develop a healthier relationship with movement. This treatment team member also continues to monitor exercise behaviors to determine energy expenditure (i.e., calories burned), which impacts body weight as well as nutritional intake goals. Sadly, exercise therapists who have eating disorder expertise are rare in the field (but they are growing), which means that the registered dietitian often must fill this role of assessing and monitoring physical activity.

Assessment for Nutrition and Exercise Behaviors

The first session with a registered dietitian necessarily involves an in-depth assessment of eating habits, exercise behaviors, medical history, body weight, and eating disorder history. For eating habits it is important to establish how much food and what types of food are being consumed. This can help the registered dietitian understand how narrow food choices have become. For example, has the client become vegetarian (i.e., no meat products) or vegan (i.e., no meat, eggs, or dairy products) since he or she started their eating disorder? Does the client have certain food preferences or food allergies? It is also important to understand the variations in one's diet as well as how food intake has changed over time. Has the client been on certain diets or engaged in fasting?

Within the initial assessment, it is also important to establish a baseline for physical activity behavior. Some clients are completely sedentary whereas other individuals report engaging in excessive exercise behavior. The assessment should determine whether the client feels compelled to exercise and is able to vary the intensity and type of physical activity performed. In other words, the question should be asked, "What type of physical activity counts as exercise to you?" Clients should be probed about when they stop exercising or take a rest day. Do clients feel the need to exercise even if it means missing work, school, or other family obligations? This question allows the clinician to evaluate the priority of exercise behavior over other aspects of one's life.

A comprehensive assessment includes conducting a detailed medical history including body weight and eating disorder history. As part of this aspect of their assessment, the registered dietitian should gather information about any current prescription medications, dietary supplements, or other over-the-counter medications that may interfere with nutrition status. Clients can also be queried about their lowest and highest weight to better understand weight fluctuations that have occurred as a result of disordered eating behavior. The registered dietitian will want to understand the frequency of disordered eating behaviors including purging methods (e.g., vomiting, laxative use) and dietary restriction.

Setting Nutrition Goals for Eating Disorders Treatment

Once the comprehensive assessment has been conducted to understand eating disorder history and dietary behavior, the problem areas should drive the development of nutritional goals for the client. They should be personalized for the individual and will differ depending on diagnosis and severity of the eating disorder. Anorexia nervosa and bulimia nervosa will need to have different goals initially, but ultimately it is important for all clients regardless of their eating disorder diagnosis to focus on the development of a positive and healthy relationship with food. Specifically, clients with anorexia nervosa will likely have goals specific to gaining weight to achieve a healthy weight for their age and height. Because individuals with anorexia nervosa commonly are resistant to gaining weight or maintaining their body weight at a minimally normal weight for age and height, they should be assessed for any acute medical complications. The early stages of the restoring weight for clients with anorexia nervosa require constant monitoring for possible complications (e.g., heart problems) that can be associated with refeeding syndrome. There is a risk for refeeding syndrome during the early phases of reintroducing food to clients, specifically carbohydrates, resulting when the body adjusts from a catabolic to anabolic state. Refeeding syndrome is defined as a condition that involves metabolic disturbances that may occur during the delivery of nutrition to malnourished clients due to anorexia nervosa or starvation. Unfortunately, refeeding syndrome is dangerous and can be fatal due to rapid changes in electrolyte imbalances or fluids among clients who are receiving artificial refeeding with the goal of weight restoration.

In order to avoid refeeding syndrome, the registered nutrition and physician will follow guidelines for managing the condition—that is, the National Institute for Health and Clinical Excellence (NICE) guidelines. These guidelines were developed in 2006 and give specific criteria to determine clients who are "at risk" for developing refeeding syndrome. Therefore, individuals who are greater than 30 percent below their ideal body weight or who have rapidly lost weight should be closely monitored for symptoms of refeeding syndrome. From a prevention standpoint the registered dietitian will likely begin nutritional support at a lower rate and increase gradually according to NICE guidelines to avoid refeeding syndrome. For example, the initial "prescribed" caloric intake for anorexia nervosa during weight restoration may begin at an extremely low level such as 30–40 calories/kilogram/day. Once the client achieves medical stability, the treatment team can recommend that caloric intake be increased gradually. Gradual safe increases in increments of 200 to 300 calories every three to four days are advised to encourage a desired gain of 1 to 3 pounds of body weight per week.

In contrast to anorexia nervosa, nutritional goals will look different for other types of eating disorders at the outset. Bulimia nervosa, which is characterized by disordered eating behaviors, may include episodes of binge eating followed by compensatory behaviors such as self-induced vomiting, excessive exercise, starvation, or the use of laxatives and diuretics. Initially, nutrition treatment for bulimia nervosa, therefore, should focus on developing goals and putting a strategy in place to reduce and prevent episodes of disordered eating behaviors of binge eating and purging. A meal plan will be designed to help the client have planned meals that allow for the balancing of one's daily intake of carbohydrates, proteins, and fats. The registered dietitian will offer nutrition education focused on the concepts of normal eating and recommended nutritional requirements. Education should also be provided to discuss the short-term and long-term physical and psychological consequences associated with binge eating episodes and purging behaviors.

For binge eating disorder the nutritional therapy approach will differ from anorexia nervosa and bulimia nervosa. Binge eating disorder features repeated episodes of binge eating that feels uncontrollable, without the presence of any purging behaviors such as those seen in bulimia nervosa. Similarly to clients with bulimia nervosa, the initial goals for nutrition treatment will involve trying to reduce binge eating episodes and developing a consistent and balanced eating plan to follow. Unfortunately a major challenge of binge eating disorder is the tendency to employ chronic dieting behavior—periods of restriction or eating only certain types of food—which increases the risk for binge eating episodes. Therefore, nutrition education for binge eating disorder should include a discussion about the negative aspects of chronic dieting. Binge eating disorder can lead to numerous medical complications due to weight gain associated with binge episodes such as obesity, heart disease, hypertension, type 2 diabetes, and hyperlipidemia. These consequences should be addressed as part of nutritional treatment.

Meal Planning as Nutrition Treatment

For all types of eating disorders the early part of nutrition therapy should focus on stabilizing acute medical complications, stopping and preventing further weight loss (and weight gain for binge eating disorder), and changing eating behaviors to include increasing food intake or decreasing binge eating and/or purging behaviors. Regardless of the eating disorder diagnosis, the intention of implementing meal planning is to help the client to begin eating in a systematic manner throughout the day that involves a variety of foods to comprise a well-balanced diet. A secondary purpose of meal planning is to reduce the guesswork around meal times, which can help to reduce anxiety and allow clients to feel a sense of being in control at meal time. Although meal planning should not represent a permanent solution, having a constructed meal plan can offer comfort to clients and can initially break the cycle of dieting and restricting followed by binge episodes. The registered dietitian will tailor actual meal plans to meet individual's weight gain, stabilization, or loss requirements, as well as food preferences (as much as possible). However, clients will be discouraged from limiting any foods from their diet unless there is a documented food allergy. As discussed, meal plans will provide a balance of carbohydrates, proteins, and fats, as well as vitamins and minerals. Finally, one's nutritional status, medical conditions, current dietary intake, growth, and physical activity need to be taken into account when determining one's overall nutritional needs for meal planning purposes. Meal planning is determined in several ways including using an exchange list or system, consulting the United States Department of Agriculture (USDA) Food Guide Pyramid, and calorie counting.

The *exchange list* refers to a system used for meal planning to organize foods according to the proportions of carbohydrates, proteins, and fats they contain. The exchange system was originally conceived as a way to help individuals who have diabetes manage their consumption of carbohydrates, sugars, and fats. Having too much sugar, for example, could send someone with diabetes into shock. Further, the registered dietitian provides portion sizes for each food based on caloric content. Alternative food options are offered, which can be substituted without altering the overall caloric consumption or the proportion of protein, carbohydrate, and fat content. This meal planning approach has been popularly implemented in the treatment of eating disorders. Its appeal comes from having a prescription or eating plan for introducing a balanced diet that is based on scientific properties. In this case, a meal plan is constructed for the client that details how many exchanges he or she needs from each food list. Flexibility in food choices is constantly encouraged, but the client is comforted in knowing that regardless of which food item overall caloric consumption will be the same.

Another important resource to guide nutrition therapy is the Food Guide Pyramid. This USDA resource was initially developed to educate the general public about getting in all of the food groups into one's daily food intake. Originally foods were categorized into six basic groups and recommendations about how many servings should be consumed were given. The original Food Guide Pyramid was updated in 2005 in order to add physical activity into recommendation and to attempt to individualize the recommended caloric intake for each individual. Eventually, in 2011, MyPlate replaced the Food Guide Pyramid/MyPyramid to offer a powerful visual of a plate to show portions needed for a healthy diet. Although this was designed to help average Americans to eat healthy foods like fruits and vegetables (and minimize foods with little or no nutritional value), MyPlate can also be incorporated into nutrition education for treatment of eating disorders given the focus on getting food from each category onto one's plate. Encouraging healthy meal patterns that include diverse foods as symbolized by MyPlate provides a strong message around developing and maintaining a sustainable and healthy lifestyle choice for all human beings regardless of eating disorder status.

Because clients with eating disorders are often resistant to giving up control over food intake and tracking process, calorie counting may be used as a way to ease them into other nutritional approaches like the exchange list. *Calorie counting* refers to a nutritional treatment approach used initially to engage client and understand caloric deficiencies as present. Registered dietitians may view calorie counting as a last resort approach to addressing the relationship with food as it emphasizes the number rather than the quality or content of food. Moreover, the sole or continued use of calorie counting for determining meal planning needs may lead to a poor distribution of nutrients in the diet and will not address the underlying psychology around one's relationship with food. Therefore, other nutritional approaches such as the intuitive eating philosophy should be offered as quickly as possible to help clients with eating disorders reset their mindset around food.

Intuitive Eating Philosophy

Intuitive eating represents a well-known non-dieting approach to eating that philosophically is well aligned with a healthy and positive relationship with food and supports recovery from an eating disorder. Specifically, *intuitive eating* refers to returning to a time in one's life when eating behaviors were entirely based on physiological cues of hunger and fullness. In other words, decisions around eating are not made with respect to what one "thinks" he or she should be eating (in way of portion sizes or caloric content) but rather whether one is hungry or full. Intuitive eating helps individuals move away from emotional eating that is based on decision around stress. Usually stress eating may involve foods high in fat or sugar, and consumption is made without consideration for one's level of hunger.

It usually takes time to get back in touch with internal cues that are based on biology. For clients with eating disorders, food rules and attempting to discipline their eating have taught them to largely ignore and resist feelings of hunger. Therefore, clients are encouraged to listen to their bodies to notice hunger cues again. The registered dietitian will educate clients on this nutritional philosophy built on the concept of recognizing and listening to one's biological cues with regard to making food choices. They will reinforce the idea that by intuitive eating an individual can merely have his or her internal signals guide food selections without guilt or ethical dilemma.

Another important principle of intuitive eating is the encouragement of diverse foods in one's diet. Like other meal planning strategies discussed previously, having a range of food types is helpful. The intuitive eating philosophy takes this notion a step farther by stating that there are no good and bad foods. Therefore, a person has complete power to eat whatever food the body is craving. While this concept may be controversial initially, dietitians have found that when people can take the power back from food they can actually stabilize their weight. In some cases wherein intense emotional eating has resulted in binge eating episodes, individuals who successfully incorporate intuitive eating may actually lose weight.

It should be emphasized that intuitive eating can be taught during the weight restoration process; however, the focus at that phase should be gradual reintroduction to foods. It will likely take several months or longer for individuals with anorexia nervosa, bulimia nervosa, and binge eating disorder to have the ability to detect hunger and fullness cues. However, nutrition therapy and thinking about eating in a new way teaches a positive approach to making decisions around food.

Nutrition therapy is not limited to increasing caloric intake and weight restoration. Eating disorder individuals have a variety of disordered food beliefs and behaviors. It is essential that individuals are challenged to evaluate their food rules and behaviors. Individuals will often use their eating disorder to avoid certain foods or food groups. Food challenges are used to allow the individual an opportunity to confront his or her distorted thoughts associated with all foods.

Determining Healthy Body Weight in Eating Disorder Treatment

When a registered dietitian develops the nutritional goals and sets up a meal plan, it is vital to determine the appropriate target body weight for a client. Various formulas and charts can be consulted to determine an ideal body weight for one's height and age. In making decisions regarding an individual's target weight range, the treatment provider should consider the client's weight history, body composition, genetics, growth state, and physiological state. Some commonly used formulas include the body mass index, the Hamwi equation, and the Metropolitan Life Insurance weight chart.

The body mass index, which is commonly referred to as one's *BMI*, is calculated in a straightforward fashion to assess one's tendency to be having a healthy weight, overweight, or obese based on height and weight measurements. The drawback of BMI is that it considers all body weight equally regardless of whether it is fat tissue or muscle. Another problem is that BMI does not consider one's body type or frame (i.e., bone structure) when making determinations about whether someone is overweight. Therefore, what is a healthy BMI for one person can look emaciated on someone with a large bone structure? BMI is calculated by dividing weight (kg) by height (m^2). These standards indicate that an individual is considered to be underweight at a BMI of less than 18.5 kg/m^2. In adults, a BMI of 17.5 kg/m^2 is generally accepted as 85 percent of ideal body weight. BMI is often used in insurance-related decisions about the appropriate level of care for someone with an eating disorder.

Another method that has been used to determine one's target body weight is called the Hamwi equation. In this method, height and frame structure are taken into account. For men, 106 pounds for the first 5 feet plus 6 pounds for every inch over 5 feet. For women, 100 pounds for the first 5 feet plus 5 pounds for every inch over 5 feet. About 10 percent is then added or subtracted if one has a small or large frame.

Finally, the Metropolitan Life Insurance weight charts have been used to determine a desirable weight for adults for increasing their longevity. These weight charts involve identifying an ideal weight for one's height and frame size. The height value is estimated with consideration for shoes and clothing.

Ideal weight charts, formulas, and absolute BMI values need to be used with caution in children and adolescents. Because children and adolescents continue to grow, target ranges must be fluid to adjust as this growth occurs. Importantly, target body weight ranges should not be determined using a single formula or chart. Multiple factors need to be considered including weight history, familial weight history, body composition, and physiological and cognitive functionality, as well as body weight prior to the onset of one's eating disorder. Due to natural fluctuations in weight, it is best to recommend a target weight range, rather than an absolute weight.

Weight Restoration in Nutrition Therapy

Before any real progress can be made in treatment for one's eating disorder, weight restoration must occur. Being at a dangerously low body weight serves as a barrier to productive counseling sessions and puts the client at risk for ongoing health consequences. Weight restoration may involve both solid foods and liquid nutrition support. Namely, liquid supplementation should be implemented when (1) a client fails to gain necessary weight despite a reintroduction of solid foods, (2) the body weight is dangerously low and could be life-threatening, (3) decompensating psychological state or cognitive impairment, or (4) a client refuses to consume any solid foods. Liquid nutrition support is provided orally as a supplement or using a feeding tube (i.e., enteral nutrition). Liquid supplement drinks like Boost can be used along with the reintroduction of solid foods but should be weaned once food intake from solid foods is sufficient to meet the caloric demands for the day.

Sometimes, in order to achieve necessary nutrition intake for proper weight restoration, the use of tube feeding is required to complement the use of other means for getting necessary nutritional support. The use of a feeding tube provides liquid nutrition directly into the body via the stomach or nasal cavity so that it can eventually reach the gastrointestinal tract. Enteral nutrition is usually delivered to the body throughout the day or may be administered at night. The other possibility is the use of *bolus feedings*, which refers to the infusion of a high volume of liquid nutrition supplement (i.e., 500 ml or less) directly into the stomach within a short time period (i.e., fewer than 30 minutes) several times during the day. The use of continuous feeds may be avoided, since one's appetite is adversely affected, and clients will refuse to eat food orally due to poor appetite. As a last resort when severe malnutrition has occurred, parental nutrition is employed and involves an intravenous feeding process to deliver nutrients to the body. However, this invasive feeding method can expose the client to a greater risk for infections and medical complications. Clients who are actively restoring body weight or who are undergoing nutritional supplementation should avoid physical activity entirely to avoid undermining weight and nutrition goals. However, other clients who have been stabilized should begin to address their relationship with physical activity so that meal plan adjustments can be made in tandem.

33. How should a dysfunctional relationship with exercise be addressed in eating disorder treatment?

Because a large portion of clients who have eating disorders may also exhibit exercise dependence issues (i.e., abuse of exercise as a purging method), it is critically important to address one's relationship with exercise in a treatment setting. Feeling compelled to engage in a rigid exercise regimen to expend calories is a common feature among many individuals with an eating disorder. Although historically, patients who were hospitalized with anorexia nervosa were put on bed rest and ceased to exercise or be physically active during treatment, within the past few decades, clinicians have realized the utility of exercise as a form of adjunct therapy.

Specifically, exercise has been shown to effectively treat mental health conditions such as depression and anxiety. Given that these mental health disorders are often common among clients with eating disorders, there is promise for integrating exercise into a comprehensive treatment plan. However, a stigma has persisted among clinicians around having clients with eating disorders engage in exercise. They fear that including physical activity in a program will sanction unhealthy behaviors. Moreover, there is a realistic concern that physical activity will be counterproductive to and undermine the pursuit of weight restoration goals. However, recently, eating disorder treatment programs and clinicians have embraced the use of exercise in a "prescribed" fashion—that is, controlled and limited ways within a comprehensive treatment approach once clients have been medically cleared.

One key to success has been having a detailed plan in place to supervise and monitor physical activity. Only certain types of exercise should be introduced initially after a thorough assessment of overexercise behaviors and types of exercise that have been abused. For example, running is commonly abused among individuals with eating disorders due to the high caloric expenditure and weight loss potential, but forms of tai chi or relaxation yoga may be a good starting point. The topic of exercise should not be taken lightly as overexercise is one of the biggest predictors of relapse from an eating disorder.

Types of Exercise in Treatment

The most common evidence of exercise within a treatment setting is the inclusion of relaxation forms of yoga and stretching classes within a residential program. There has been research to suggest that yoga can be used as an effective intervention with eating disordered clients to teach a variety of skills such as mindfulness, stress reduction, and breathing. However, it is important to note that yoga classes out in the community may not be suitable for individuals struggling with eating disorders. In fact, power yoga and "hot yoga" may be triggering for clients who feel compelled to exercise with the motive of burning calories. Instead yoga classes in the relaxation form can be used to promote gentle stretching, deep breathing, and meditation and to develop a greater awareness of one's body. Within the treatment setting, yoga instructors can be trained to use key words or verbal cues to promote compassion for one's self and body as well as to avoid triggering words around body parts.

Another alternative to cardiovascular forms of exercise that may be beneficial and can be incorporated during eating disorder treatment is the use of resistance training. Resistance training through the use of Dyna-Bands, free weights, or machines can promote confidence around strength. Once again, strength training should be prescribed with special note to number of repetitions and amount of resistance. Whenever possible supervision of exercise session is more ideal than having clients exercise on their own. Clients should focus on how their body feels rather than attaining a specific number of repetitions or weight, to help them practice having a more healthy and positive relationship with exercise.

As mentioned earlier, cardiovascular activities like running may be discouraged while an individual is undergoing weight restoration. Some light walking may be allowable, but monitoring is important to avoid counterproductive caloric expenditure from overstrenuous exercise sessions. Attention should be given to proper form and stopping if any pain is experienced. Self-reported exercise in an outpatient setting is difficult to monitor or trust, so having an exercise buddy may be indicated.

Sports and play may be used to remove attention from calorie-burning aspects of exercise. Having an outside goal (e.g., scoring a point by shooting a basket) may help distract client from the traditional exercise mindset. Playing novel games that are unfamiliar can be particularly helpful to individuals with eating disorders. These activities are a great tool to teaching a new psychological mind-set around movement.

Exercise Education

The most essential ingredient when dealing with dysfunctional exercise as part of eating disorder treatment is *education* about one's relationship with physical activity. The numerous benefits of physical activity beyond caloric expenditure, weight loss, and appearance should be emphasized so that the client can begin to adopt additional motives for exercising. Clients should be encouraged in therapy sessions to explore their primary motivation for exercising and when it started. Was there a time in their life when exercise was playful, enjoyable, and flexible? It is important to understand that one's relationship with exercise is quite personal, and there may be resistance to changing one's routine.

Clients should be encouraged to broaden their perspectives around what "counts" as exercise in attempts to address rigid and narrow exercise routines. For example, individuals with eating disorders may perceive running to be exercise whereas walking does not get counted (or reported to one's therapist) despite burning calories. In order to have a healthier relationship with exercise, clients should employ a variety of types of physical activity. Ideally, individuals are able to rediscover enjoyment associated with human movement. This fun factor is often lost once physical activity becomes compulsory, and a client feels obligated to engage in excessive exercise patterns.

Using an intuitive exercise approach, clients should be retrained to tune into how their bodies are feeling (i.e., kinesthetic sense) while they are moving. Personal trainers who have received training about how to work with eating disorder populations may be helpful in demonstrating proper form for movement including heel-to-toe movement during walking and how to maintain proper posture during resistance training. Using one's senses to be more present and mindful during exercise is an important step. Mindful exercise can be incorporated during a therapy session to cue clients to focus on smells, sounds, and sights on a walk around the building. Ultimately individuals will constantly need to reflect on their inner voice around exercise. Recovery and being recovered is represented by having a positive and healthy relationship with food, exercise, and themselves.

34. What can someone who is entering into eating disorder treatment expect?

Individuals who take the important step of seeking treatment for their eating disorder report feeling mixed emotions. Typically the dysfunctional behaviors have been kept private and hidden from others for a long period of time. For this reason, the assessment session where the intake and initial interview takes place can feel like one is metaphorically "coming out of the closet." For some individuals, sharing one's struggle can be associated with a tremendous amount of relief in the way that water can be allowed to flow once again when a large obstacle (e.g., boulder) is removed. Finally being able to "come clean" about one's behaviors, negative thoughts, and feelings can be liberating. Having a skilled clinician ask relevant questions and provide nonjudgmental stance can feel incredibly validating.

On the other hand, for other individuals, this experience of airing one's dirty laundry can feel like being exposed in a deeply uncomfortable way. Experiencing a strong level of emotional vulnerability can be so difficult for some individuals that they want to discontinue their pursuit of treatment and recovery. In other words, it seems like the better option is to remain disordered in one's eating and in a familiar zone rather than to open oneself to risk and exposure. Hopefully the person who is entering into eating disorder treatment has been encouraged and supported by a family member or trusted friend who can help him or her work through this early challenge and perceived barrier to treatment.

The actual process of being in treatment for an eating disorder varies greatly depending on level of care, one's geographic region, and whether a specialty eating disorder provider delivers the care. However, a shared piece to seeking treatment is the continued emotional ups and downs one can expect to experience throughout the journey. Initially the treatment will likely focus on abstaining from disordered eating behaviors such as restricting, purging, and binge episodes. In an outpatient setting, when slips (i.e., disordered eating behavior) occur, they will be discussed in treatment. Therapist and client will work through how to develop ways for dealing with intense emotions and replacing disordered eating behaviors with another coping strategy that is healthier and less dysfunctional.

In an outpatient setting, many things will remain the same for the client who is undergoing treatment for his or her eating disorder. He or she may continue to work or attend school. The client will likely continue in his or her current living situation whether it be with family members, roommates, or a significant other. The client will schedule therapy visits with a mental health counselor, as well as a dietitian and physician. The client may likely be encouraged to build a social support network and to communicate needs to others around what is helpful in the therapeutic process. For example, if a client is living with his or her family, it will be important to establish whether family members are to act as the "food police." As the name implies, being the "food police" often denotes a level of monitoring and oversight regarding the types and amount of food consumed. While this is generally discouraged, there are certain instances—usually those that involve insurance not covering a higher level of care (e.g., residential)—that may warrant training family members to take on a staff role in the short term. Family members will also need to be educated about what is an appropriate level of exercise during this initial stage of treatment. Some clients will find the need to relinquish some of their responsibilities in order to focus on treatment. They may reduce work hours, take medical leave, or take the semester off from school. However, each case should be considered on an individual basis.

Athletes and other performers face special challenges when they venture into treatment for their eating disorder. The treatment team must determine the benefits and drawbacks of having the client continue participation in his or her sport or performance-related activity (e.g., playing an instrument, dance). For some athlete clients, the decision will be made for them to be benched from sport while weight restoration and medical stabilization occurs. They will likely feel isolated from their teammates and identity as an athlete or performer. For other athletes and performers, it can be advantageous to remain engaged in their "normal" routine. This structure of having practices and competitions may provide motivation to get better as well as a built-in social support system. It must be emphasized that this cannot be a one-size-fits-all approach when determining the best course of action for sport or performance participation. For residential settings, some will require that athletes, employees or students discontinue participation during their stay.

In a residential setting, clients will likely experience a living arrangement similar to a dorm-style setting. In this level of care, meal plans, medications, and bathroom time will be monitored around the clock to prevent eating disorder-related behaviors. It is likely that this level of supervision may be perceived negatively at first. Clients often report feeling that staff does not trust them to be independent and make sound decisions. Staff are trained to respond in an empathetic but firm way. Staff have been trained to understand that the struggle is intense for clients and they will be resistant to change. Individuals in a residential setting will be faced with a full program that includes structured activities as well as weekends that may be less structured. Depending on the philosophy of the treatment center, clients may not see their families at first, may see them infrequently, or may participate in family counseling sessions. In a residential setting, clients will be interacting with new people—staff, treatment providers, other clients, and possibly a roommate. Certain personality dynamics are likely to develop during their residential stay. Even adults may find this setting challenging given that freedoms they take for granted, such as when they eat, how much or little they eat, and how much they sleep, will not be available to them. Some clients have described the situation as feeling like they are in a prison with food police, exercise police, and hall monitors. Generally, clients adapt and come to understand how the supervision is designed to help them with their treatment process.

In an inpatient setting, clients will expect to find a hospital-like setting. The focus will be on stabilizing vital signs and managing medical symptoms. Often clients are under doctor's orders to be on bed rest, which is extremely challenging. The goal is to spend as little time as possible in the inpatient level of care to move to more therapeutic activities within lower levels of care (e.g., residential treatment setting), where the "real" work can begin to take place.

35. What support groups are available to help people who have an eating disorder?

Support groups typically refer to groups in the community that are available to provide a platform for interacting with other people who are undergoing the same struggle or have a similar problem or addiction. Support groups originated with substance use disorder and addiction populations with organizations such as Alcoholics Anonymous and Narcotics Anonymous. However, in recent years eating disorder-specific groups have also popped up, especially in larger cities. The purpose of eating disorder support groups is to allow for individuals with eating disorders to receive support from others during their treatment (as a supplement to their therapy with a licensed professional). Secondarily, eating disorder support groups can be beneficial when someone is in recovery and wants to remain mindful of functional and healthy coping methods. Eating disorder support groups can be especially useful given the secretive nature of disordered eating behaviors. Having others in the same group that can identify with challenges, triggers, and struggles is validating. Verbalizing—that is, putting words to one's problem—in a nonjudgmental setting allows for an individual to be accountable to his or her behaviors.

There are several types of support groups, but most are free to the public. Some are closed groups, which means that they are only accessible by certain individuals, while others are open and advertise for anyone who might like to attend. *Intact groups* refer to those support groups that have the same members for a certain duration to ensure consistency and accountability. This allows members to obtain greater depth and avoid having to adjust to the infusion of new members constantly. Other groups, like the commonly publicized anonymous groups mentioned earlier, are founded on the principle of being open to all whenever the person is ready to seek support. Therefore, people have the opportunity to engage at any point of their treatment and recovery.

Eating disorder support groups may be affiliated with a treatment facility to assist with transition and recovery of clients upon discharge. Usually alumni from treatment centers are encouraged to attend regular support group meetings to stay accountable to their recovery and maintain connected to a network of people who understand their journey.

Additionally, some eating disorder treatment centers offer support groups for friends and family members of clients. These support groups are designed to provide family members and friends with a place to discuss their stressors and struggles related to supporting an individual with an eating disorder. Commonly there are financial stressors among family members when insurance does not cover treatment. There is also stress related to the feelings of powerlessness on how to help their family member. These support groups allow for the chance to meet others in their situation and to give education around how to best provide support while taking care of themselves in the process.

Eating disorder support groups can also be aligned with associations like the National Eating Disorder Association or the National Association of Anorexia Nervosa and Associated Disorders (ANAD). For example, ANAD offers support groups for both individuals with eating disorders and separate groups for family members of people with eating disorders.

Twelve-Step Support Groups

Twelve-step programs are frequently available as an option for support groups in many cities. Twelve-step programs are self-help programs created to assist in the recovery from various types of addictions and compulsions. Problems such as dysfunctional family dynamics that are tied to addictions are also addressed within the context of these support groups that were designed to provide a judgment-free zone for addicts.

In 1935, the first type of 12-step support groups, Alcoholics Anonymous (AA), was founded by two "recovering" alcoholics (i.e., sober and living a lifestyle that promoted and maintained their sobriety). The AA program was developed to support people like the founders who were actively pursuing a recovery lifestyle. The purpose of these support groups was to provide a peer group atmosphere to allow for accountability in recovery. Since their origin, the 12-step programs have been adapted for many other support groups for compulsive and other behavioral problems, such as Narcotics Anonymous, Gamblers Anonymous, and Debtors Anonymous. There are purportedly over 200 self-help programs across the world. Although people with eating disorders can attend the widely available 12-step AA groups that offer a similar addiction focus, some communities also have support groups specific to eating disorders. Twelve-step groups developed specifically for eating disorders and for persons struggling with disordered eating include but are not limited to Overeaters Anonymous (OA), Eating Disorders Anonymous (EDA), and Anorexics and Bulimics Anonymous (ABA).

OA has been around longer than any of the eating disorder-specific 12-step support groups as it was founded in 1960. Groups are offered across the United States and exist in more than 20 countries. The purpose of OA is to help members understand that their eating behavior (i.e., binge episodes) is actually reflective of an addiction to food in the way that alcoholics crave alcohol as their substance of choice. Compulsive eating is discussed with the understanding that emotional eating in response to a variety of stressors must be stopped to break the cycle. The OA support groups offer a similar premise to other support groups around working through 12 steps and acknowledging a higher power. This is the most commonly available 12-step group specific to eating disorders, but its focus on compulsive overeating resonates with individuals suffering from and recovering from binge eating disorder. However, individuals who are struggling from bulimia nervosa or individuals who engage in compulsive overeating may also find the support groups useful. Although some individuals with anorexia nervosa may attend in the absence of other support groups specific to eating disorders being available, they may not immediately relate to the members of OA and will need to focus on their individualized recovery. The approach on recovery is the same for all members of OA regardless of symptomology or one's particular eating disorder diagnosis.

Several decades later, the ABA, another 12-step group for disordered eating, was founded. ABA, which was established in 1992, modified the 12 steps and program of AA to tailor for use with persons who struggle with anorexia nervosa or bulimia nervosa that want to develop a healthy relationship with food and eating. The ABA program is intended for people with anorexia or bulimia to meet other people struggling with the same disorders. ABA, like other 12-step programs, represents a valuable resource to complement a comprehensive treatment approach to addressing eating disorder concerns. More recently, the EDA was founded by members of AA in Phoenix, Arizona. This 12-step program, which started offering groups in 2000, was intended to help individuals with eating disorders be supported in their recovery. EDA states that the goal for members is balance as demonstrated by a healthy relationship with food and eating as opposed to abstinence, a common feature of other 12-step programs (e.g., Gamblers Anonymous and AA).

Common across all 12-step support groups is the philosophy that working through addiction is a lifelong process. Although 12-step groups are not affiliated with a particular church or religion, there is an emphasis on acknowledging a higher power. A strong focus within recovery is healing through one's spiritual journey. These support groups are free of charge and open to anyone who wants to develop healthy eating patterns. Typically these peer-run support groups are facilitated by someone who is in recovery from an eating disorder rather than a licensed professional counselor. Both 12-step programs and clinicians generally concur that support groups should not replace one's therapeutic work with licensed professionals. Instead support groups can provide a supplement to existing therapy with a multidisciplinary treatment team.

36. Are there alternative or complementary treatment methods available to address eating disorders?

Complementary and alternative medicine (CAM) therapeutic approaches have gained in popularity with many illnesses and mental health disorders including eating disorders. Although many people have never heard of integrative health, they are likely aware of the idea of holistic health or alternative medicine. In fact, the holistic movement has been taken by storm in many hospitals, universities, and medical schools. The goal of CAM or integrative health as a philosophy and therapeutic approach is to treat the mind, body, and spirit concurrently rather than treating physical symptoms in isolation. Research studies have demonstrated findings that show a promising relationship between the brain, immune system, one's emotions, and disease state. Incorporating an integrative approach for use with eating disorder treatment can be implemented with the multidisciplinary treatment team that is positioned to support treatment and recovery aims. The residential treatment for eating disorders is particularly well positioned to offer these alternative approaches to therapy, such as acupuncture and massage therapy; however, CAM can be introduced at any level of care. It should be noted that the role of complementary therapies should be used as adjuncts to a comprehensive treatment plan to include traditional psychotherapy, nutrition support, and medical monitoring and stabilization. Examples of CAM include but are not limited to meditation, massage therapy, acupuncture, and energy psychology.

Meditation to teach mindfulness skills is used to help clients center themselves in the present moment and to bring awareness to every aspect of daily life. A common example of how to teach mindful eating involves using a raisin or chocolate kiss to experience eating in a new way that involves as many senses as possible. Clients are asked to smell the raisin and notice its texture before popping it in their mouth. Then clients are asked to chew slowly and meaningfully to fully experience the taste. This type of activity helps teach awareness and brings a level of connectedness to eating that is often absent among people who are chronic dieters or who engage in restricting behavior.

Meditation and Breathing

A variety of strategies can be taught to increase one's awareness and ability to be mindful. Basic meditation techniques, such as Transcendental Meditation, can be conducted in a seated or slightly reclined position using repetitive phrases to stay centered over a 20-minute period. Breathing is an important skill to employ to help individuals with eating disorders to calm their mind and anxiety and come back to present focus. For example, the combination of using focused breathing and simple yoga postures can help to relax and get reconnected with one's body to help with emotional regulation. Using a meditative form of breathing that involves deep breathing for a specified number of counts can help bring attention back to the body and one's breathing, as well as calming the mind. Practice of meditative breathing is critical so that this healthy coping skill can be used in times of stress to help relax and refocus rather than being triggered to engage in disordered eating behaviors. Another type of meditation called *guided meditation* can be used as part of treatment to walk clients through a scenario while in a relaxed state. This script is used to help visualize fears associated with meal time or to re-experience the uncontrollable urge to binge or purge. This is a powerful technique to be able to help client feel triggers without engaging in the dysfunctional behavior. Clients can be encouraged to think of an alternative outcome from disordered eating or replacement coping strategy that can be used.

Therapeutic Massage

Another popular form of CAM is the use of therapeutic massage as an adjunct to traditional therapy. Therapeutic massage is commonly referred to as *therapeutic touch* and can be considered a controversial form of treatment due to the physical touch component. Given that clients with eating disorders may report having a history of trauma or abuse, the use of this powerful technique must be considered carefully and on an individualized basis. Some residential treatment programs have included massage as part of a comprehensive treatment program. Because clients with eating disorders can be resistant to change and may not do well in traditional therapy, using CAM may be a helpful adjunct. One study found that therapeutic massage was helpful in reducing anxiety, depression, eating disorder symptoms, and negative body image among individuals with eating disorders. Interestingly, a connection was found between women with anorexia nervosa and a deprivation of physical touch during childhood. Therefore, providing a safe way of introducing a positive form of nurturing touch for these individuals can be extremely therapeutic. Ultimately teaching clients how to use self-massage can be an empowering way to provide clients with a tool to use as a healthy coping strategy for addressing intense emotions and times when they feel triggered. Self-massage can also be used to demonstrate appropriate boundaries of touch.

Acupuncture

Acupuncture has been a therapeutic approach that does not involve medication to address many types of diseases and conditions including eating disorders. Acupuncture, which dates back thousands of years, is the practice of using needles to insert into specific sites on the body to form pressure. Acupuncture represents a natural form of Chinese Medicine that supports a philosophy that all illness is the result of an imbalance between one's mind, body, and spirit. The goal of acupuncture is to restore health by readjusting and balancing energy by healing physical and emotional distress. Acupuncture has been found to be effective in alleviating food allergies, digestive problems, and food cravings, as well as disordered eating behaviors.

Yoga

Yoga is another activity that can encourage mindfulness. Although considered a physical activity or exercise intervention, yoga has also been classified as a complementary form of therapy. Research studies have demonstrated the positive impact of yoga on decreasing stress levels, improving concentration, teaching mindfulness, and helping a person connect with his or her body in the present. Yoga has been shown to be a positive adjunct to a comprehensive treatment program for eating disorders.

37. Can an individual outgrow his or her eating disorder?

Not usually. Eating disorders can affect people of any age despite the commonly held belief that only teenagers worry about how they look and have eating disorders. While it is true that prevalence rates are likely higher for children and adolescents than other age brackets, people do not merely "grow out" of their eating disorder when they become older. Although adolescents and college-aged individuals are considered at risk for eating disorders more than other age group, only 40 percent of eating disorders occur in people between ages 15 and 19. Ultimately, a person of any age can suffer from a poor body image or develop an eating disorder. Some studies show women experience intense body dissatisfaction during certain life milestones such as pregnancy, giving birth, or menopause. Pregnancy may be associated with bodily changes that contribute to stretch marks, weight gain, or other conditions. There is a large focus on losing the "baby weight" once a woman has had her baby. People of all ages can be identified as struggling with negative body image and disordered eating behavior. Therefore, education is important so individual cases that fall outside of the adolescent age bracket are not overlooked.

Living in a culture that values beauty and appearance impacts people at every age and can make growing older much more difficult. Further, this myth that people graduate from eating disorders or outgrow body dissatisfaction has not been shown to have validity in research that study people across the life span. One study that examined women 20 to 80 years of age found that women in the United States ages 40 to 60 were the most dissatisfied age subgroup of all women. This might partially be explained by the existence of a major milestone for women: menopause. *Menopause* refers to the time that marks the end of a woman's menstrual cycle based on the natural biological process. The average age for menopause, which is determined once a woman has gone 12 months without a menstrual period due to age-related changes and not some other medical reason (e.g., anorexia nervosa), is 51 years of age This phase in life can result in increased weight gain and body fat around the waistline. Menopause tends to cause body weight changes because of the increased storage of fat tissue and hormonal changes.

Although there is a common misconception that, as people mature, they stop caring about the shape and size of their bodies, the reality is that the triggers remain in our weight-focused culture. Our sense of insecurity related to our body and its flaws linger. The research suggests additional concerns, such as changes related to body weight and skin texture may contribute to a higher dissatisfaction in middle-aged individuals.

Individuals cite wrinkles, increased hair growth in undesired areas, and weight gain as age-related factors that occur naturally but tend to negatively affect one's body image.

38. Is it possible to be fully recovered from an eating disorder?

The concept of being in recovery versus having the opportunity to be fully recovered has been controversial within the field of eating disorders. Generally, in the addictions area it is commonly agreed upon that people who have struggled with alcoholism or a substance use disorder are always in recovery (rather than recovered) for their entire life. Twelve-step support groups like Alcoholics Anonymous espouse this philosophy for its members and use associated language of being "in recovery." This even applies to individuals who have abstained from the use of their object of addiction over a number of years, who present little to no risk for relapse. However, the philosophy is based on the belief "once an addict, always an addict" and that the potential to abuse again is always there. Having this belief of "recovery" reinforces a need to continue to attend 12-step support groups and other programming throughout one's life and to be watchful of any emerging triggers.

For eating disorders, professionals have clearly delineated recovery from being recovered. Eating disorder organizations such as the National Eating Disorder Association have advocated that being recovered is possible. This message of having the ability to strive for being recovered can offer hope to individuals who struggle from eating disorders. Eating disorder clinicians and researchers also promote this overarching philosophy in literature and in their clinical practice that individuals can be "recovered from" an eating disorder rather than "in recovery." Being recovered symbolically represents past tense, which is more empowering for individuals and encourages the disengagement from one's eating disorder identity. Furthermore, working toward full recovery or being recovered denotes optimism and the ability to improve one's condition.

The recovery language specific to one's journey with eating disorders usually refers to an absence of disordered eating symptoms or behaviors. This would include all disordered eating behaviors ranging from restricting food to purging or engaging in binge eating episodes. Ultimately in order to meet the definition of being "recovered" a person who has an eating disorder history should be completely indistinguishable from individuals who do not have eating disorders (or a history of disordered eating). Being "fully recovered" is identified by meeting several specific criteria including: (1) not meeting the *Diagnostic and Statistical Manual of Mental Disorders, Fifth Edition* (DSM-5) diagnostic criteria for an eating disorder any longer; (2) not having engaged in any disordered eating behaviors (e.g., vomiting, binge eating, exercise to purge, binge eating episodes, restricting) for at least three months; (3) maintaining a body mass index (BMI) of 18.5 or more; and (4) demonstrating a score within what is considered normal for one's age on eating disorder screening tools. Another important feature to be considered "fully recovered" from an eating disorder involves demonstrating the ability to reduce the potential for slips synonymous with minimizing the risk for relapse. It is estimated that around half of all individuals with eating disorders are able to fully recover from their disorder, while about one-fifth of individuals with anorexia nervosa and bulimia nervosa remain disordered and continue to meet *DSM-5* criteria for an eating disorder. Less information is available on the recovery rates for binge eating disorder and other feeding disorders like avoidant restrictive food intake disorder.

Clinicians have recognized the term "partial recovery" to reflect a state in which an individual can resist from actively engaging in disordered eating behaviors and having normal and acceptable BMI scores for one's age while not meeting the psychological criteria necessary for full recovery. For instance, in the treatment setting that provides a controlled environment and plenty of structure many clients are successful at alleviating disordered eating symptoms. Staff monitor meals and bathrooms, which does not happen in outpatient setting beyond discharge from a supervised setting. However, even though clients in this setting may be free of symptoms, they still admit to struggling from intense body image concerns and dissatisfaction with body parts. Because individuals who are in partial recovery admit that they continue to experience negative body image and eating disorder triggers, they are at increased risk for relapse once the structure of a treatment setting is removed.

As mentioned previously a commonly held belief related to addiction is that an individual who has a history of addiction will always be an "addict" and will remain in "recovery" and that recovery represents a lifelong process. Eating disorders differ from other addictions in that it is impossible to abstain from eating. Therefore, individuals with eating disorders must develop a healthier and more positive relationship with food in order to recover and ultimately be fully recovered from an eating disorder.

Other Questions

39. Who are some famous people with eating disorders?

Anorexia nervosa leapt into the public spotlight in 1983 when Karen Carpenter, a popular American singer and drummer, died from heart failure attributed to an eating disorder. It has been reported she was criticized for her weight during her teenage years. A diet evolved into a full-fledged eating disorder resulting in excessive weight loss. The entertainment industry is associated with certain appearance expectations, and many celebrities have admitted they suffered from eating disorder to stay slim and get roles. While famous people are no different from the rest of the population, they do have to endure their weight struggles in the spotlight. The media can be merciless in body-shaming celebrities for having a *bad body image day*. To fight back, some celebrities are speaking out about the powerful negative message we send to children about self-worth when it is tied to body weight, shape, size, and appearance.

Famous people can provide a voice to the need for awareness, prevention, and early intervention for eating disorders. In addition to Karen Carpenter, numerous celebrities have struggled with eating disorders. A few famous people who are detailed here include Lily Collins, Troian Bellisario, Lady Gaga, Kate Winslet, Angeline Yap, Tallulah Willis, Zayn Malik, and Christy Henrich.

Lily Collins is an actress who used her prior experiences as a teenager who struggled with an eating disorder to inform her starring role in a film that features eating disorders, *To the Bone*. In the movie, Collins, who is a 27-year-old actress in real life, depicts an emaciated individual who suffers from anorexia nervosa and seeks help at a residential facility. She has been open with her battles in order to remove stigma from the topic and to advocate for individuals with eating disorders.

Troian Bellisario, who stars in the television show *Pretty Little Liars*, admitted to a struggle with anorexia nervosa. She attributes her concerns with eating to her dysfunctional relationships with parents and a desire to please everyone in her life. Bellisario also linked her inability to express emotions in a healthy way with a tendency to use self-destructive behaviors like restricting food. Ultimately, the actress gave in to the pressure to be happy all the time, despite experiencing immense sadness.

Stefani Joanne Angelina Germanotta (aka Lady Gaga) has revealed her struggles with anorexia and bulimia nervosa that started in high school. She desired a small and skinny physique despite having a naturally curvy figure. Interestingly, the effects of bulimia nervosa negatively affected her singing voice, reinforcing the detrimental effects stomach acid from frequent vomiting can have on vocal cords. Throughout her pop career, Lady Gaga has continued to promote positive body image and serve as an advocate for others struggling with eating disorders.

Kate Winslet, who is a British actress, has discussed her struggle with body weight issues throughout her life. She suffered from weight-related bullying in high school due to being overweight and had the nickname "Blubber." As a well-known actress in the movie *Titanic*, she was recognized for her curves. After having struggles with disordered eating when she was younger, she has refused to give in to the Hollywood pressure to be thin and emaciated.

Angeline Yap became famous for being Miss World Singapore. She admitted to struggling with anorexia nervosa for over seven years. Throughout her eating disorder her body weight became dangerously low, and she became isolated from her friends and family members. She also felt hopeless and depressed, which led to self-harming behavior and multiple suicide attempts. A wake-up call came in the form of losing her friend who was also suffering from anorexia nervosa. Since that time she has received treatment for her eating disorder and slowly turned her life around.

Zayn Malik has made headlines after revealing in his new book that he suffered from a serious eating disorder during his One Direction days. The singer is one of a number of celebrities who have opened up about struggles with eating disorders over the years in the spirit of raising awareness and encouraging people who do suffer to speak out and seek help. Boy band members have expressed pressures to meet particular body ideals and maintain lean physiques.

Christy Henrich may not be considered a celebrity by Hollywood standards, but the former Olympic gymnast has brought attention to the problem of eating disorders in sports. Henrich, who was a competitive gymnast, was purportedly told by judges that she would be well served to lose weight in order to improve her performance and Olympic chances. Her coach was rumored to have referred to her body as a "Pillsbury dough boy" during a practice session. These comments are thought to have triggered restrictive eating and a downward cycle of eating disordered behavior. Her anorexia nervosa has been blamed for her dangerously low weight and eventually for her death in 1992. Henrich serves as a reminder of the impact of pressures to lose weight in sport environment and how negative comments can contribute to the development of disordered eating and eating disorders.

40. What are "pro-ana" and "pro-mia" websites, and how do they relate to eating disorders?

A troubling social media trend that actively promotes dysfunctional dieting behaviors and eating disorders is represented by pro-ana and pro-mia websites and online communities. Initially they existed as independent, freestanding websites that would pop up and be removed before showing up at a different HTML address. Currently, many social media sites such as Facebook, Myspace, Tumblr, and Instagram unknowingly host pro-ana and pro-mia support groups. *Pro-ana* refers to a movement or effort to promote anorexia nervosa and associated behaviors. On the other hand, pro-mia websites actively celebrate bulimia nervosa. It is counterintuitive to think individuals may be actively championing unhealthy behaviors and mind-set around food.

Pro-ana and pro-mia websites often employ *thinspirations* or motivational messages or images that revolve around staying disciplined in one's diet or food restriction. These photos may feature extremely thin or bony women who serve as the inspiration to stay strong. In addition to offering emaciated images online, blogs and forums provide an opportunity to post discussion threads to encourage interaction between members. Messages are frequently posted that stigmatize gaining weight or having curves. Recommendations are provided to coach visitors to the website on how to handle parents who act as the *food police* and how to resist the urge to eat fattening foods. Crash diets and recipes may be offered. Additionally, suggestions are provided about proposed purging methods, such as using laxatives and enemas. Finally, ways to ignore hunger pangs are discussed on the websites.

These pro-ana and pro-mia online communities support disordered eating and reinforce an individual's distorted thoughts surrounding food and body image. These websites and support groups can be especially triggering for people who struggle with eating disorders and receive the opposite message in treatment. Eating disorders are extremely secretive and isolative in nature, so the support, validation, and anonymity provided by these online communities and websites are a dangerously enticing combination. Interestingly, many of these sites claim not to actively promote eating disorders. However, it is clear that the images and messages are geared toward the encouragement of dieting and disordered eating behavior and the celebration of ultrathin bodies. Pro-ana and pro-mia sites can be particularly damaging as they provide a sense of community and social support for individuals who are already vulnerable.

41. Can eating disorders be prevented?

Although the importance of prevention is frequently given lip service, much stronger attention is needed to address eating disorders in light of the strong emphasis on the obesity epidemic. Because society's focus is preventing obesity and diabetes, the message that is often conveyed is that we all need to lose weight, restrict food, and fear weight gain. Moreover, the message of healthy physical activity can become translated into promoting an excessive form of exercise that can become dysfunctional and part of an eating disorder. Specifically, we need to tweak our obesity prevention message to promote a positive health focus for all individuals *regardless of their weight, shape, or size.* Programs that teach children and parents to develop healthy relationships with food, exercise, and their bodies can help prevent not only obesity and overweight (which can include binge eating disorders) but also other feeding disorders. These programs can take place in existing classrooms in middle school and high school, as well as after school. For example, teaching a positive health approach in health classes can include a focus on eating healthy and incorporating a wide range of foods into one's diet. Further, the downfalls of adopting a dieting mentality should be illuminated for students who may start a diet quite innocently. In addition to providing programming to students, individuals who work at schools (e.g., athletic trainers, teachers, coaches) should be educated about how to detect disordered eating behavior early, how to find local resources available in one's community, and how to refer individuals when necessary. Several key steps can be taken to prevent eating disorders.

Our society's focus on dieting (as discussed in question 19) contributes to an obsession over what we eat and how we look. This preoccupation leads us to get stuck in an endless cycle of yo-yo dieting and other compulsive behaviors designed to sculpt our body closer to our perceived ideal. Unfortunately as has been mentioned, dieting can progress into disordered eating and clinical eating disorders. Therefore, this dieting mentality should be discouraged, and a focus should move away from beauty as the only valued attribute within our culture. It is critically important that eating disorders be prevented given that they are associated with numerous adverse health consequences. Further, treatment of eating disorders can be extremely challenging. Most experts agree helping individuals avoid the factors perpetuating eating disorders (like starvation and nutritional deprivation) is crucial to prevent eating problems in the first place.

De-Emphasize Body Weight and Appearance

Adults and family members need to recognize their important position as role models of a positive health approach. Comments they make about their own bodies or others will have a negative impact on children and teenagers. Placing a large value on how one looks will also be spotted by younger family members or students. Whenever possible scales or other bodily measurements as a means of testing should be avoided in schools or health promotion contexts. Eliminate "biggest loser" types of contests or campaigns that encourage weight loss as the goal or measure of success. If mirrors are present in classrooms, they can be covered to prevent an emphasis on gazing at one's body or comparing one's body to others. Although it is easy to get sucked into the dieting mentality and desire to change one's body weight, shape, or size, we need to fight the temptation to participate in our normative culture.

Avoid Body Shaming and "Fat" Comments

Parents and other adults can serve as role models of positive body image messages. Therefore, they should avoid body-shaming themselves or others. The use of the word "fat" and other negative versions should be avoided. Jokes about a person's weight or size may have perilous impacts on one's body image. In fact, studies have shown that even indirect comments about weight can have detrimental effects on the body image of people around those messages. Likewise it is important to remember that children and adolescents may be the victims of weight-related teasing or bullying at school or in the home environment. If a problem is detected, it is important to discuss in a genuine and caring way. Keeping the secret will not help anyone. It is anticipated that denial will be the initial response from someone who is struggling from an eating disorder or being bullied for their weight or appearance, but it is still important to identify concerns and offer support. Having some local resources available is likely to be helpful once the individual is ready to seek treatment.

Going on a "family diet" can convey a message of "good" and "bad" foods. Instead promoting an intuitive eating approach—that is, eating when one is hungry and stopping when one is full—is a healthy approach. Diverse foods in one's diet should be encouraged. Displaying a positive approach to health and well-being represents being a strong role model for body image.

42. How can I get involved in the cause to raise awareness about eating disorders?

Every February, the National Eating Disorders Association (NEDA) hosts an eating disorder awareness week. Communities around the country (and world) are encouraged to organize local activities to support this event. You can raise awareness by organizing an event or by participating in local programs at a university or library in your community. In the fall, NEDA Walks are scheduled across the country to bring awareness to eating disorders. You can get involved by walking to show your support for the cause or by donating to a NEDA Walk. You can also use your pocketbook to donate to eating disorder research by supporting NEDA, International Association for Eating Disorder Professionals, or Academy of Eating Disorders. Several foundations engage in fund-raising to raise monies for scholarships so that someone can undergo treatment for his or her eating disorders.

Another important aspect of raising awareness of eating disorders is through advocacy and lobbying. Specifically, advocacy is needed to help improve insurance coverage for eating disorder treatment. In its current form, if insurance covers treatment, it is typically at a lower level of care than is required. Additionally, a person is unlikely to get the entire treatment duration covered by his or her health insurance. Many eating disorder organizations in the community are engaged in some form of advocacy: whether through resources, events, information, and more. Some of these organizations include the NEDA, the Academy for Eating Disorders, the Eating Disorders Coalition, Project Heal, the Alliance for Eating Disorders Awareness, and Maudsley Parents. Depending on what niche of the eating disorder community interests you, such as policy, treatment, insurance coverage, or media, there are several ways to be involved. Consider reaching out to an organization that interests you about volunteer and outreach efforts. Advocacy can be something as simple as sharing resources, making phone calls, or participating in an event; every effort makes a difference.

Case Studies

The following case studies are intended to provide "real-life" examples of how an eating disorder can present itself in a variety of situations. In this section of the book, five scenarios that depict different eating disorder case examples are presented. Each case illustration will describe the details of a fictionalized account of an eating disorder example before providing the recommended treatment and recovery plan to address the problem.

CASE 1: ANOREXIA NERVOSA

Barbie, who is now 15 years old, was referred to as the "skinny kid" growing up. She would try on her kids' clothes and proudly fit into them for years beyond their appropriateness for the age, but it felt like a badge of honor. She was the kid that could eat anything, and people would say she was like a "tapeworm." "Where does the food go?" people would ask her. When Barbie hit puberty she noticed that her body suddenly developed in some areas, and she felt like her body was a lot more soft and squishy than it was ever before. Her peers notice and make comments that she is "finally growing up." Adults also make comments telling her that she has a "cute little curvy figure." These comments even when intended to be compliments make Barbie feel quite self-conscientious and overly focused on her body. Bottom line is that Barbie is deathly afraid of gaining weight. Barbie decides she must take matters into her own hands. She creates a highly disciplined meal plan for herself that cuts out all animal products, fats, and sugars. She also decides to fast for two or three days of the week, which involves consuming less than 500 calories on those days.

Barbie's parents are concerned because they have observed changes in her diet and unwillingness to join them at the kitchen table for dinner. She also has an excuse to skip dinner, whether it is finishing up homework or going to sleep early. When she is in a position that she must come to dinner, Barbie often sits without eating anything beyond a few roasted vegetables and drinks a glass of water. She seems to have some food rituals of cutting her veggies into small pieces before chewing them very slowly. Barbie is also the last one to finish her plate even though she has the smallest amount of food. She has given her family a direct explanation for her food restriction. Specifically, she reports that she is detoxing and apparently wants to cleanse her body from toxins. But her parents notice that the restrictive food regimen is resulting in rapid weight loss for Barbie. Barbie's mother recently became aware that Barbie no longer has a menstrual cycle. Her clothes are hanging off her body, and she has dropped two sizes in pants over a matter of months.

Despite this weight loss that is evident to everyone around Barbie, Barbie expresses discontent with her body. She reports feeling fat when anyone ever mentions her losing weight. She seems to view herself in a different way that is distorted from reality. More troubling still is that Barbie seems to seek inspiration from ultrathin models in magazines and on the Internet. She has joined several forums online that seem to encourage her to remain disciplined in her fasting routine. Her mom discovered Barbie pouring over visual images of emaciated bodies that were portrayed with protruding collar bones and clearly identifiable rib cages.

In addition to the drastic weight loss, Barbie is showing some other signs of poor eating habits. She has developed a bit of fine hair on her arms and face. Her cheekbones seem to be more prominent. She seems to bruise easily without really having much impact or contact with a surface. Barbie also displays difficulty sleeping and demonstrates low energy. She reports frequent headaches and stomach pain. Given the medical problems, Barbie's parents think it is appropriate to bring her into the physician for treatment. What should they do?

Analysis

It is common for parents like Barbie's parents to start by taking the individual to a medical professional in order to address medical symptoms. However, it is important for them to report the other circumstances that are contributing to weight loss such as changes in diet. It is likely that the family physician will detect the common signs and symptoms of an eating disorder. Barbie meets all of the telltale signs of anorexia nervosa. She has lost weight—likely she is at a much lower weight for her height than she was in the past. Although losing one's menstrual cycle is no longer a required criterion, it is yet another signal that one's body is not functioning as it should. Her restrictive behavior fits the bill along with her recent shift to vegetarianism. Moreover, she continues to have an intense fear of gaining weight. Her reports that she is overweight demonstrate a body image distortion that is consistent with anorexia nervosa.

Once Barbie is diagnosed with (or at least suspected to have) anorexia nervosa, she will be referred for a more comprehensive eating disorder assessment. At the assessment, Barbie will be asked questions about her eating history as well as how her body weight has changed. She will also be interviewed about all of the symptoms she is experiencing. Because her body is experiencing some physical signs from malnourishment, she will need to address the medical aspect of eating disorder within treatment. She will also be encouraged to pursue mental health counseling to explore body image issues and negative self-esteem. A dietitian will work with her to help on gradual weight restoration to achieve a healthy weight for her natural body structure and height. She may need to engage in meal planning to understand how to incorporate more diverse types of food into her diet. Finally, she may benefit from a more structured environment—that is, residential treatment center—for her eating disorder. This will allow her to work with a multidisciplinary team to stabilize her weight while tackling psychological issues around food and her body image. In this environment she will have the opportunity to be monitored as she is relearning how to eat regular meals. She will also receive support during meals from trained staff who understand what she is going through. Likely this encouragement to eat more diverse foods and ultimately gain weight will induce anxiety, and working through the emotional component will be critical for her ongoing recovery. Developing a new identity that is not so deeply tied to being a "skinny person" will be important for her progress especially to avoid being triggered moving forward.

CASE 2: EXCESSIVE EXERCISE AND MUSCLE DYSMORPHIA

Richard, who is 32 years old, spends a disproportionate amount of time at the gym. He focuses on being able to lift as much weight as he can on the bench press and squat machine. He also has added ambitious goals for himself to include 20 pull-ups without assistance. Recently he has joined a CrossFit class, which has been the extra push he was looking for in his workout regimen. Richard has noticed that it takes him more time to get a decent workout, and he must always increase weights and repetitions. He also has become increasingly rigid in his categorization in what he counts as exercise. For example, running on the track or outside does fit the bill for cardiovascular exercise, but he does not consider walking his dog to be exercise.

Richard actively compares his body to others at the CrossFit gym. He wants to be the most lean and muscular. He feels insecure when others can do more repetitions of a given exercise or when he feels fatigue and must stop a particular exercise or obstacle. When Richard looks in the mirror he picks himself apart. His eyes immediately go to his midsection, which he describes as doughy and out of shape. He feels that his shoulders are underdeveloped and that his chest is concave. He experiences intense body dissatisfaction, which drives him to work out even more. Lately he has been tempted to add Creatine to his supplement routine. He already adds protein supplementation to smoothie drinks twice a day. He tries to restrict fats and carbohydrates. He primarily consumes lean proteins. Sometimes he will splurge on a piece of chocolate cake or peanut butter cookie. Then he feels the need to exercise even more strenuously than usual to compensate for the calories consumed.

But he feels like he needs an extra boost to help him get over the hump. It is noteworthy that Richard also engages in body-checking behaviors that involve pulling at his skin and touching his muscles. He tries not to deviate from his lifting routines, as he fears he will lose muscle quickly. He already feels like he is underweight and lacks muscle.

Richard's body dissatisfaction and self-loathing are apparent in his efforts to hide his body by wearing baggy clothing. He has strategically added tough-looking tattoos to his arms to give the illusion that he is larger than he feels on the inside. He thinks about his size, weight, exercise, and diet in an obsessive fashion. His increasingly longer work-outs have meant that he has joined multiple gyms in the area to avoid judgment from others. He now misses spending time with his family at night and on the weekends. He avoids his guy friends because they just want to drink beer and watch sports, which is too sedentary for him. He no longer has a social life or much identity beyond the workouts that monopolize his time. Richard is terrified that he is gaining fat and increasing his body composition. To make matters worse he recently injured his shoulder and is having to work out in spite of immense pain.

He is unsure what to do given his obsession with working out and his unhappiness with his body. What should Richard do?

Analysis

Clinicians might suggest that Richard's behavior fits the bill for excessive exercise. He displays a dysfunctional relationship with exercise, because he feels compels to exercise strenuously. This description of needing more exercise to feel that he is accomplishing something aligns with the concept of exercise tolerance—that is, he is developing a tolerance for high standards of exercise and must exercise more to get the same effect.

In addition to experiencing exercise tolerance, Richard spends more time engaging in exercise at the expense of other activities or obligations in his life like spending time with family members and friends. His day is increasingly revolving around exercise as evidenced by multiple memberships to various gyms and reporting increasingly more rigid exercise regimen. He is experiencing injuries from overexercise, yet he is unable to take time off from exercise.

Although Richard clearly shows the signs of exercise addiction or having a dysfunctional relationship with exercise, he also displays the telltale signs for muscle dysmorphia. Muscle dysmorphia is defined in the literature as being dissatisfied with one's body and exhibiting a distorted view of one's size. That is, in Richard's case, others view him as muscular and fit, whereas he feels that he is too small. He is also experiencing shame associated with his physique that has resulted in wearing baggy clothing. These body image concerns have helped drive an obsession with a grueling exercise routine coupled with an overly strict dietary program.

Experts would recommend that Richard see a mental health professional to work through his body image concerns related to wanting to be larger and more muscular. Goals should involve developing a more positive perception of self while decreasing negative behaviors like body-checking and body-shaming. He will likely need to work on his overall self-worth and discover how his dysfunctional exercise behavior is tied to feelings of inadequacy. He is striving for an unrealistic ideal of being extremely lean while still muscular that is affecting his eating, exercise, and personal life. In counseling Richard will need to address the excessive exercise behavior and examine his motives for physical activity. He will need to work on changing his mind-set around exercise to expand what counts as physical activity. He will also be encouraged to add activities that he considers to be enjoyable while trimming back the time he spends in the gym. His clinician should confront the time he is missing with his friends and family members in social setting and explore whether other areas are being affected (e.g., work obligations). Knowing that he has already injured himself, the clinician will need to work quickly to help him address his compulsion to exercise through pain. He will need to be encouraged to take a rest day from exercise as part of a more balanced and moderate approach to physical activity. Using exercise as a purging method represents disordered eating behavior. Therefore, the clinician should explore whether other disordered eating behaviors are present. Referring Richard to a dietitian may be helpful to ensure that he is getting adequate food intake and to help him get more variety in his diet. Furthermore, a healthcare professional should provide Richard with guidance to reduce his consumption of protein powders and replace with whole foods that can provide the necessary nutrients as part of an overall healthy diet.

CASE 3: BINGE EATING DISORDER

Billy is the 46-year-old father of seven children. His kids range in age from 16 months to 23 years old. All but one of his sons and daughters still live in the home. His wife, whom he met in college, is a stay-at-home mother now. Their shared values of religion and having a big family have served them well. Generally he would describe his relationship as "good," but he finds himself wondering if there is more (or should be more). His cravings for something beyond his current life situation seem to come out through his love for food. In other words, he eats to fill a void in his life or to soothe his emotions as they arise.

One of his self-identified faults is that Billy has never felt able to communicate his emotions. It is especially difficult for him to express negative feelings of any kind. Instead Billy tends to stuff his emotions down deep inside and put on a happy face to hide his true feelings. His family is never the wiser, but increasingly Billy feels dissatisfied with his life. He finds himself being annoyed at little things at home and work. His coworkers make a joke and he laughs, but he finds himself feeling irritated on the inside. When his daughter neglects to pick up her shoes from the door and he trips over them, he finds that he becomes angry—overly upset—and raises his voice. When their 16-month-old son cries, he wants to scream or run away from responsibility. He knows that his bad mood is not healthy. Whenever he becomes frustrated it usually leads to a binge eating episode. For Billy this means consuming whatever food is available quickly before anyone can catch him in the act. At home this is challenging with such a large family, so Billy finds himself going through a drive through at a fast-food restaurant. In order to avoid being overly recognized, Billy will alternate between McDonald's, Burger King, Hardee's, and Arby's for his binge meals. He usually gets foods that are easy to consume and feel like "comfort eating." For example, milkshakes and French fries are common binge foods.

When Billy is having a binge eating episode, he feels unable to stop himself. There is a point in time during the overeating that he feels temporarily at peace. But that moment is short-lived, and he feels compelled to eat beyond the point of feeling stuffed. He immediately feels guilt after the binge eating episode. Billy works to cover his tracks by hiding any evidence of his binge eating. He will drive around to find a trash receptacle and to eliminate any wrappers before he gets home. He does not purge after his binge eating episodes but often feels sick to his stomach. These binge eating episodes have been occurring several times a week for almost a year. Billy has gained weight—he is unsure how much weight—but likely over 20 pounds. He was not a small man before, but now he is unable to fit into a regular seatbelt. When he travels in a plane, he feels extremely uncomfortable in the airline seat. He knows that his overeating is a problem and that he is not happy but is unsure of where to start. What should Billy do?

Analysis

Billy should seek the support of a mental health counselor to work through his issues. A primary goal of treatment should be to work on communicating one's emotions in a healthy way so that he is able to express his feelings to others. He will likely be diagnosed with binge eating disorder as he meets all of the clinical criteria. Binge eating disorder is now a formal eating disorder with its own category in the *Diagnostic Statistical Manual of Mental Disorders*. He may seek treatment for his binge eating disorder from an eating disorder specialist in order to reset his meal planning. He has likely lost touch with his biological cues of hunger and fullness due to the binge eating episodes that were emotionally driven. He will want to move away from emotional eating and would likely benefit from learning about the intuitive eating philosophy. Intuitive eating will help Billy assess his hunger level before he eats so that he will not allow himself to get to an empty tank. He will also want to have a plan for meals so that he is not tempted to go and pick up binge foods. He should be evaluated by a medical professional to determine if he is suffering health consequences from his binge behavior and overweight status.

Some therapists may say that Billy is facing a "midlife crisis" as evidenced by his feelings that he is not fulfilled. Whatever he is experiencing,

Billy will want to re-evaluate his life and whether he can add some new activities into his day. He will need to learn new coping skills to replace the binge eating episodes. Furthermore, he will want to address his feelings of irritability. They are likely an outgrowth of not expressing his emotions. Therefore, healthy communication is key to Billy's progress as he continues down the path of recovery.

CASE 4: SUBCLINICAL EATING DISORDER

Elise, who is 58 years old, finds herself single after getting a divorce from her long-time high school sweetheart. She was dismayed to learn that her husband of several decades had been cheating on her with his administrative assistant. She realizes she was the last one to know partially because of her denial. She did not want to believe that she might find herself single again. The telltale signs of infidelity were there— perfume on his suit coat, late nights at the office, and hushed phone conversations. Even when she learned of the affair, Elise desperately tried to keep the marriage intact. She offered to participate in couples counseling and to change her appearance. Her former husband reported being "madly in love" with his coworker, and they have now moved to Rincón, Puerto Rico. Due to Elise's high-powered career as an attorney, she never had children. She realizes she is very much alone and hardly knows how to change a light bulb or complete the taxes. To make matters worse, Elise has not been in the dating scene since high school. She feels she must have a dramatic change in her life to start this new chapter.

Her first step is to go on a diet. Her diet starts innocently enough—she tries reducing the amount of sugar and salt she consumes. She realizes she can cut out other foods like breads and pasta to get a faster result. Her friend, Sally, who recently lost a bunch of weight after becoming frustrated with the quintessential postmenopausal weight gain, tells her some dieting tricks. She takes laxatives (six per day) to stay regular and then skips meals when she cannot have a healthy option. Sally also recommends that Elise start participating in Orange Theory classes to get within her target heart rate zone.

Initially Elise feels energized and is elated when the weight begins to melt off. But then she feels like she has hit a wall and weight remains stuck in one place. She continues to focus on calories in and out in an almost obsessive manner and starts feeling negative side effects from the laxatives. She experiences dehydration and finds it unpredictable when she will need to relieve herself. Even Sally tells her she might want to cut back on laxatives and eat a bit more. Her neighbors who have noticed her rapid weight loss bring her casseroles and assume it is tied to the relationship loss. By focusing (i.e., obsessing about) on her bodily appearance and by engaging in dieting, Elise is able to achieve a sense of being in control despite the chaos in her life.

Unfortunately, Elise feels insecure about her appearance and the fact that she feels "past her prime." She has spent hundreds of dollars to get a new haircut and to cover her gray hairs. She is getting facials to make her skin look more youthful in appearance. She is wondering whether she should consider CoolSculpting to remove the last of her weight around the midsection region. She blames menopause and physiology for a slowing metabolism. Her body seems to absorb the calories. She is also buying special foods from Jenny Craig in attempts to control her weight. She weighs herself religiously, and her mood swings based on the number on the scale. She often has crying spells where she uncontrollably wails and feels down in the dumps. What should Elise do?

Analysis

Elise's story demonstrates that even when people do not have a full-blown eating disorder that meets all of the clinical criteria, there can still be cause for concern. Further, this case study illustrates that developing disordered eating behaviors even in the short term can have consequences such as fatigue and dehydration. Consequently, this example also clearly shows that disordered eating patterns can occur in people who are not in their teenage and college years. Elise, who is in her 50s, is struggling with a number of emotional issues including the disordered eating. It is important to point out that the impetus for her dysfunctional behaviors was her marital discord.

This case clearly exemplifies that disordered eating is not usually about food. In Elise's case, she is suffering from depression associated with her relationship problems. Her coping response is dysfunctional and involves using food to regain a sense of control. Although she acknowledges feeling poor esteem around her appearance and aging, must of this sense of inadequacy stemmed from her relationship turmoil. It is recommended that Elise seek the help of a licensed professional mental health provider. Ideally a holistic approach can be employed to address her problems around relationships, mood, and disordered eating. First, she needs to confront her feelings around the loss of her relationship whatever they may be—anger, loneliness, depression, anxiety, or a combination of many different emotions.

It will be important for her to understand the way she is linking eating behavior to a response to her relationship difficulties and emotions. She will want to eliminate the use of laxatives and work with a dietitian to develop a more balanced and regular eating plan. She will likely want to incorporate many types of foods rather than limiting her intake to Jenny Craig brand items. Although Orange Theory exercise classes can be a healthy way to manage stress, she may want to also add some other forms of enjoyable physical activity. Perhaps she likes gardening and working out in the yard, which can be considered physical activity. Taking a dance class, meditation, or yoga class could also be a way to engage in an activity that encourages mindfulness and is enjoyable. Ultimately, she will want to learn some healthy coping strategies. Elise's biggest step is developing a new identity that does not include wife of her former husband. Although this will be a challenging step to take, it is necessary. She will want to identify some new activities and ways that she will develop herself as a whole person. She will also be encouraged to expand her social support and friend network. Maybe she can join a book club or service group to meet new people in her community. Having some new friends is critical given that some of her "old friends" were aligned with her couple status.

CASE 5: ATHLETICS AND EATING DISORDERS

Jamie, who is 18 years old, made the college tennis team. She was excited for the transition and to move out of her home state of Maryland to go to a small town in South Carolina. She met her roommate at the honor's college event and stayed in contact prior to the move. They coordinated about what colors for bed comforters and dormitory furniture. Now that she has arrived to campus, Jamie feels overwhelmed. Her tennis team has lots of practices, which is fine, but there are also social activities. The coach encourages the team to eat together and to do activities outside of practice like yoga classes and movie nights. She finds it exhausting to spend so much time with her teammates, and it does not allow her much time for anything else. Her homework is slipping, and given that she wants to complete the honor's program, her classes are more challenging than many of her teammates' classes. She has already taken the necessary Advanced Placement exams to waive some of the general classes.

She also feels overwhelmed with having a full range of menu choices and food options on campus. She no longer has a parent looking over her shoulder to tell her not to eat a particular food or to avoid soft drinks. She finds herself drinking Mountain Dew from cans in her dormitory vending machine in order to stay up to study. She also eats junk food like donuts and cheese crackers when she feels overtired the next day. Her roommate is super understanding and shares her food. She always has a full supply of homemade cookies and brand name granola bars since her family lives in the next town over. Jamie often finds herself binge eating some of her roommate's treats. She sometimes eats when she is not even hungry. Afterward, she becomes fearful of gaining weight from eating a sugary food or too many calories, which leads her to engage in a compensatory method. Lately she has gone down the hall to purge by using vomiting. One of her teammates taught her this technique after a night of drinking (in order to feel better). When she was in high school, Jamie would purge by using excessive exercise when she ate a forbidden food or too much of something. Jamie does not like to run, but she will punish herself when she overeats or has "bad food."

Jamie feels so stressed about academics that she is taking caffeine pills to stay up at night. She has found that these same pills can be used for dieting purposes, and she now uses them in place of food. Unfortunately, the pills leave her feeling jittery, and she feels like she crashes a few hours later. She has trouble sleeping when she is able to and ends up feeling really drained. She is concerned that her eating and sleeping problems, coupled with her high level of stress, will hurt her performance in tennis and in class. What should Jamie do?

Analysis

It is normal for a new college student to experience stress during his or her transition from high school to the college environment. In Jamie's case she has moved to a new state and has newfound freedom away from her family. After being successful in high school sports and academics, she is in an entirely new place. She shows evidence of being a high achiever in her desire to pursue the honor's program while maintaining her status as a student athlete on a college campus.

She faces high demands from her sport team that extend beyond the typical practices and training. She will need to evaluate what is mandatory and required versus what she might be able to opt out of for her team. In addition to her teammates on the tennis team, being at a new school Jamie is also meeting all new people and friends. The counselor will likely validate her feelings of being overwhelmed in this setting. It is not surprising that Jamie is unsure how to balance her time effectively and how to maintain a regular eating and sleeping schedule. She may benefit from going to the counseling center at the university. They can assess her for an eating disorder given her identified purging behaviors used to compensate for eating certain foods. Especially of concern is the excessive exercise and the introduction of vomiting to eliminate unwanted food.

Jamie will need to develop a regular eating schedule and strive to maintain a consistent sleeping schedule. She will need to eliminate the use of caffeine pills to help her body get more in a natural rhythm. This may mean that she will need to work on a schedule to figure out times to slot in study sessions. It may be recommended that Jamie develop some friendships outside of tennis so that she has a strong support system. She will be encouraged to identify some healthy coping skills and strategies to promote self-care behaviors to replace disordered eating. For example, is she able to do some activities (e.g., listening to music, working on a puzzle) that she enjoys to calm down from the stress of studying and sport?

Glossary

Acid Reflux: A digestive disease or condition in which the stomach acid or bile irritates the food pipe lining causing heartburn. Also referred to as *gastroesophageal reflux disease* when acid reflux occurs more than twice a week.

Acupuncture: Uses thin needles that are inserted into the skin with the intention to restore health by readjusting and balancing energy.

Alexithymia: Defined as the inability to identify and describe one's feelings.

Anorexia Nervosa: A mental disorder frequently referred to as "self-starvation syndrome" in which individuals are underweight and restrict their dietary intake in a way that nutrient demands are no longer met, which negatively affects a variety of bodily systems.

Anxiety: Refers to having perceived threat and negative emotions associated with a future competition or event.

Binge Eating Disorder (BED): Defined as recurring episodes of binge eating and one of the clinical eating disorders found in the current version of the *Diagnostic Statistical Manual of Mental Disorders*.

Body Mass Index (BMI): A measure of body mass based on a person's height and weight. National Institutes of Health defines a person's weight according to the BMI as normal weight, overweight, or obesity.

Bulimia Nervosa: A mental disorder classified as one type of clinical eating disorder that is characterized by negative body image, binge episodes, and purging methods.

Cholecystokinin (CCK): A hormone that creates a sense of satiation.

Chronic Fatigue Syndrome (CFS): A debilitating and complicated disorder characterized by extreme fatigue and cannot be explained by an underlying medical condition.

Clean Diet: A simple concept that refers to eating whole foods or minimally processed or as close to their natural form.

Comorbidities: The presence of two or more diseases or disorders often referred to as *co-occurring*.

Congestive Heart Failure: Results when the body is unable to effectively pump blood into the body.

Cortisol: A hormone released in times of stress.

Dehydration: Caused by the depletion or lack of intake of fluids, or by restriction of carbohydrates and fat.

Dental Caries: Refers to tooth decay or cavities associated with some people with eating disorders.

***Diagnostic Statistical Manual of Mental Disorders, Fifth Edition* (DSM-5):** The 2013 edition of the American Psychiatric Association's *Diagnostic and Statistical Manual of Mental Disorders* classification and diagnostic tool.

Dyspepsia: Indigestion or discomfort in the upper middle part of your stomach. Eating disorder patients frequently report gastrointestinal symptoms.

Eating Disorders Coalition (EDC): A special interest eating disorders group created in 2000 that is dedicated to advocating for more legislative action within Congress.

Eating Disorder Inventory (EDI): A self-report questionnaire used to access the presence of characteristics associated with eating disorders created by David M. Garner et al. in 1984.

Energy Psychology: Based on the premise that painful emotional, spiritual, and physical symptoms are the consequence of disruption in the energy system. It is practiced in many different forms beyond acupuncture, including meridian-tapping techniques, Thought Field Therapy, acupressure, Emotional Freedom Technique, and touch therapy.

Enteral Nutrition: Liquid nutrition support using a feeding tube and usually delivered to the body throughout the day or may be administered at night.

Esophageal Rupture: A tear in the path through the throat to the stomach (esophagus), generally happens during severe vomiting and chest pain.

Exchange List: Refers to a system used for meal planning to organize foods according to the proportions of carbohydrates, proteins, and fats they contain, which was originally conceived as a way to help individuals who have diabetes manage their consumption of carbohydrates, sugars, and fats.

Exercise Dependence: Defined as when exercise becomes excessive and has a negative effect. Specifically, when the exerciser or athlete feels compelled to exercise or experiences guilt around not exercising, the benefits associated with a moderate approach to exercise begin to dissipate.

Flatulence: An excessive accumulation of gas that collects in the digestive system.

Food Cravings: Typically independent of any physiological need and are considered to be psychological in nature.

Forgiveness Meditation: Used to address anger and hurt that are directed toward the self and others and can encourage nonjudgmental acceptance of feelings.

Gum Disease: Refers to gingivitis and is caused by the irritation of the gums from the acid that results from vomiting.

Hamwi Equation: Another method used to determine one's target body weight by using height and frame structure in this measurement.

Health-Related Quality of Life (HRQoL): A multidimensional concept commonly used to examine an individual's perceived mental and physical health over time.

Hypotension: Decreased blood pressure resulting from a decrease in cardiac output, arterial tone, and effective arterial blood volume.

Inpatient: Refers to the level of care that is most restrictive and is limited to clients who require highest level of supervision.

Integrative Treatment Approaches: Refers to traditional treatment methods for eating disorders provided by an interdisciplinary team of professionals, including but not limited to primary care doctors, cardiologists, dentists, dietitians, psychotherapists, recreational therapists, and art therapists.

Intensive Outpatient: Refers to a lower level of care that is more cost-effective than residential and inpatient options. Clients typically come in for a half-day program several days per week to participate in comprehensive activities.

Intuitive eating: Refers to returning to a time in one's life when eating behaviors were entirely based on physiological cues of hunger and fullness.

Meditative Breathing: This technique is used as a relaxation component and is powerful for focusing. It works by balancing the autonomic nervous system and by drawing attention to physiological processes that can be directly experienced without being threatening.

Mindfulness Meditation: This meditation takes only a few minutes, and many people report that it has a meaningful impact on their subsequent experiences with eating by bringing awareness to every aspect of their daily life.

Mononucleosis: Also known as mono or kissing disease, which is caused by the Epstein-Barr virus and is transmitted through saliva.

Mortality: Fatality rates associated with a particular disease.

Muscle Dysmorphia: An obsessive focus on building muscles paired with a perception of being too weak can translate into unhealthy habits, such as extreme detoxification cleanses, excessive exercise at the risk of injury, low-fat or no-fat diets, and the use of anabolic substances to promote muscle growth.

National Institute for Health and Clinical Excellence (NICE) Guidelines: Developed in 2006 and give specific criteria to determine clients who are "at risk" for developing refeeding syndrome.

Neurocognitive: The functions associated with processes of the central nervous system in cognition.

Neuroepinephrine/Serotonin: The norepinephrine that provide a sense of emotional and physical satisfaction.

Osteopenia: Commonly seen in people over 50 years old that have lower than average bone density.

Osteoporosis: A bone disease associated with low bone mineral density and is represented by bone density loss of more than 2.5 standard deviations from what is considered normal for one's age.

Other Specified Feeding or Eating Disorder (OSFED): The *DSM-5* category that formerly was recognized as Eating Disorder Not Otherwise Specified in the *DSM-IV*. OSFED captures eating and feeding disorders of clinical severity that do not meet the full diagnostic criteria for anorexia nervosa, bulimia nervosa, or binge eating disorder.

Outpatient: Refers to traditional individual and group therapy for about 50 minutes each within the community.

Pancreatitis: The inflammation of the pancreas, which is the large gland behind the stomach and near the first part of the small intestine.

Parental Nutrition: Refers to a last resort when severe malnutrition has occurred and involves an intravenous feeding process to deliver nutrients to the body.

Partial Hospitalization: Refers to the level of care that includes group therapy sessions, meal monitoring, and individual work with a multidisciplinary treatment team; however, clients go to their home after the program.

Peptic Ulcers: An open sore in the lining of your stomach and/or the upper portion of your small intestine.

Prognosis: One's potential to improve from a particular condition and demonstrate favorable treatment outcomes.

Project HEAL: A nonprofit that raises money for eating disorder treatment and advocates for awareness.

Pro-Mia: The celebration of bulimia nervosa through websites and social media that can result in the perpetuation of unhealthy behaviors.

Refeeding Syndrome: Defined as a condition that involves metabolic disturbances that may occur during the delivery of nutrition to malnourished clients suffering from anorexia nervosa or starvation.

Residential: Refers to a level of care that is less restrictive than inpatient wherein the client is supervised by staff 24 hours a day and 7 days a week. In this setting clients have the opportunity to take risks and work through emotional issues in a safe place.

Restricting Food: Defined as reducing or eliminating food items from one's diet.

Spiritual Wisdom: Refers to an exercise that can help people connect to values, strengths, and a higher life purpose through inner awareness and peace.

Transcendental Meditation: Involves a sitting or slightly reclined 20-minute meditation with repetition of a personal mantra.

United States Department of Agriculture (USDA): A Food Guide Pyramid resource that was initially developed to educate the general public about getting in all of the food groups into one's daily food intake.

Yo-Yo Dieting: Involves alternating periods of liberal eating and highly restrictive eating, which may be predictive of psychological hunger and inability to rely on the physical cues for hunger.

Directory of Resources

BOOKS

Anorexia Nervosa: A Guide to Recovery

Author: Lindsey Hall and Monika Ostroff
Publisher: Gürze Books
Year: 1998
ISBN: 978-0936077321

Beginner's Guide to Eating Disorders Recovery,
25th Anniversary Edition

Author: Nancy Kolodny
Publisher: Gürze Books
Year: 2004
ISBN: 978-0936077451

Bulimia: A Guide to Recovery

Author: Lindsey Hall and Leigh Cohn
Publisher: Gürze Books
Year: 2010
ISBN: 978-0936077512

Embody: Learning to Love Your Unique Body
(And Quiet That Critical Voice!)

Author: Connie Sobczak and Elizabeth Scott
Publisher: Gürze Books
Year: 2014
ISBN: 978-0936077802

Filling Up: The Psychology of Eating

Author: Justine Reel
Publisher: Greenwood
Year: 2016
ISBN: 978-1-4408-4089-0
eISSN: 978-1-4408-4090-6

Full of Ourselves (FOO): A Wellness Program to
Advance Girl Power, Health, and Leadership

Author: Catherin Steiner-Adair and Lisa Sjostrom
Publisher: Teachers College Press
Year: 2005
ISBN: 978-0807746318

Intuitive Eating: A Revolutionary Program That Works

Author: Evelyn Tribole and Elyse Resch
Publisher: St. Martin's Griffin
Year: 2012
ISBN: 0-312-32123-6-51395

Making Peace with Your Plate: Eating Disorder Recovery

Author: Robyn Cruze and Espra Andrus
Publisher: Central Recovery Press
Year: 2013
ISBN: 978-1937612450

Making Weight: Healing Men's Food Weight, and Shape

Author: Arnold Andersen, Leigh Cohn, and Tom Holbrook
Publisher: Gürze Books
Year: 2000
ISBN: 978-0936077352

The Parent's Guide to Eating Disorders: Supporting Self-Esteem, Healthy Eating, and Positive Body Image at Home

Author: Marcia Herrin and Nancy Matsumoto
Publisher: Gürze Books
Year: 2007
ISBN: 978-0936077031

Psychology of Eating: From Healthy to Disordered Behavior, Second Edition

Author: Jane Ogden
Publisher: Wiley-Blackwell
Year: 2010
ISBN: 978-1-4051-9120-3

Starting Monday: Seven Keys to a Permanent, Positive Relationship with Food

Author: Karen Koenig
Publisher: Gürze Books
Year: 2013
ISBN: 978-0936077789

Unweighted Nation

Author: Jenny Conviser Jenny and Jason Conviser
Publisher: Healthy Learning
Year: 2017
ISBN: 978-1606793909

JOURNALS

Eating Disorders: The Journal of Treatment & Prevention

Publisher: Routledge
Website: http://www.tandfonline.com/loi/uedi20#.VfbBx9JVhBc

International Journal of Eating Disorders (IJED)

Publisher: Wiley
Website:http://onlinelibrary.wiley.com/journal/10.1002/(ISSN)1098-108X

Journal of Clinical Sport Psychology (JCSP)

Publisher: Human Kinetics
ISBN: 1932-9261
eISSN: 1932-927X
Website: http://journals.humankinetics.com/JCSP

Journal of Nutrition (JN)

Publisher: American Society for Nutrition
Website: http://jn.nutrition.org/

ORGANIZATIONS

Academy for Eating Disorders (AED)

11130 Sunrise Valley Drive, Suite 350, Reston, Virginia 20191 USA
Phone: 703-234-4079
Fax: 703-435-4390
E-mail: info@aedweb.org
Website: http://www.aedweb.org
Global professional association committed to leadership in eating disorders research, education, treatment, and prevention.

Academy of Nutrition and Dietetics (Eat Right Pro)

120 South Riverside Plaza, Suite 2190, Chicago, IL 60606-6995 USA
Phone: 1-800-877-1600 or 312-899-0040
Website: http://www.eatright.org/
World's largest organization of food and nutrition professionals.

American Nutrition Association (ANA)

Website: http://americannutritionassociation.org/
A nonprofit on a mission to promote optimal health through nutrition
education.

American Psychology Association (APA)

750 First St. NE, Washington, DC 20002-4242 USA
Phone: 1-800-374-2721 or 202-336-5500 TDD/TTY: 202-336-6123
Website: www.apa.org
Scientific and professional organization representing psychology in the
United States.

American Psychiatric Association (APA)

Phone: 1-888-35-PSYCH or 1-888-357-7924
Outside the U.S. and Canada: 703-907-7300
Website: www.psych.org
Organization of psychiatrists working together to ensure humane care
and effective treatment for all persons with mental illness, including
substance use disorders.

American Society for Nutrition (ASN)

9211 Corporate Blvd., Suite 300, Rockville, MD 20850 USA
Phone: 240-428-3650
Fax: 240-404-6797
Website: http://www.nutrition.org/
Nutrition scientists who conduct nutrition research and translate find-
ings into practice.

Binge Eating Disorder Association (BEDA)

637 Emerson Place, Severna Park, MD 21146 USA
Phone: 855-855-BEDA (2332) Fax: 410-741-3037
Website: http://bedaonline.com/
National organization focused on providing leadership in the recogni-
tion, prevention, and treatment of binge eating disorder.

Centers for Disease Control and Prevention (CDC)

1600 Clifton Road, Atlanta, GA 30333 USA
Phone: 800-CDC-INFO (800-232-4636) TTY: (888) 232-6348

E-mail: https://wwwn.cdc.gov/dcs/ContactUs/Form
Website: http://www.cdc.gov/physicalactivity/
Website: http://www.cdc.gov/HealthyLiving/
U.S. federal agency whose main goal is to protect public health and safety through the control and prevention of disease, injury, and disability.

Council on Size and Weight Discrimination

P.O. Box 305, Mt. Marion, NY 12456 USA
Phone: 845-679-1209
Fax: 845-679-1206
E-mail: info@cswd.org
Website: www.cswd.org
Council working to change public policies and people's attitudes concerning body weight.

Eating Disorders Coalition (EDC)

P.O. Box 96503-98807, Washington, DC 20090 USA
Phone: 202-543-9570
Website: http://www.eatingdisorderscoalition.org/
Organization that advances the recognition of eating disorders as public health priority in the United States.

FEAST (Families Empowered and Supporting Treatment of Eating Disorders)

P.O. Box 11608, Milwaukee, WI 53211 USA
Phone: 1-855-50-FEAST (USA); 1-647-247-1339 (Canada);
    61-731886675 (Australia); 44-3308280031 (United Kingdom)
E-mail: info@feast-ed.org
Website: http://www.feast-ed.org/
International organization of and for caregivers of eating disorder patients by providing information and mutual support, promoting evidence-based treatment, and advocating for research and education to reduce the suffering associated with eating disorders.

Food Nutrition Service: USDA (United States Department of Agriculture)

3101 Park Center Drive, Alexandria, VA 22302 USA
Phone: 703-305-2062

Website: http://www.fns.usda.gov/
Provides information to increase food security and reduce hunger by providing children and low-income people access to food.

International Association of Eating Disorders (iaedp)

P.O. Box 1295, Pekin, IL 61555-1295 USA
Phone or Fax: 1-800-800-8126
E-mail: iaedpmembers@earthlink.net
Website: http://www.iaedp.com/
Members and resources for international multidisciplinary groups and professionals working in the eating disorder field.

Multi-Service Eating Disorders Association (MEDA)

288 Walnut Street, Suite 130, Newton, MA 02460 USA
Phone: 617-558-1881
Website: www.medainc.org
Regional and national support network and resource for clinicians, educators, and the general public.

National Association for Males with Eating Disorders (NAMED)

2840 SW 3rd Ave, Miami, FL 33129 USA
Website: http://namedinc.org/
Provides support for males affected by eating disorders.

National Association of Anorexia Nervosa and Associated Disorders (ANAD)

220 N. Green Street, Chicago, IL 60607 USA
Phone: 630-577-1330 (helpline) or 630-577-1333
E-mail: hello@anad.org
Website: www.anad.org
Resources for people to overcome their fears and issues with eating and body image.

National Association of Student Personnel Administrators (NASPA)

111 K Street NE, 10th Floor, Washington, DC 20002 USA
Phone: 202-265-7500

E-mail: office@naspa.org
Website: http://www.naspa.org/
Organization for the advancement of student affairs profession.

National Eating Disorders Association (NEDA)

165 West 46th Street, Suite 402, New York, NY 10036 USA
Phone: 1-800-931-2237
E-mail: info@NationalEatingDisorders.org
Website: http://www.nationaleatingdisorders.org/
Nonprofit organization dedicated to supporting individuals and families affected by eating disordersNational Institutes of Health (NIH)
9000 Rockville Pike Bethesda, MD 20892 USA
Website: https://www.nih.gov/
Nation's medical research agency making important discoveries that improve health and save lives.

National Institute of Mental Health (NIMH)

Science Writing, Press, and Dissemination Branch
6001 Executive Blvd., Room 6200, MSC 9663, Bethesda, MD 20892-9663 USA
Phone: 1-866-615-6464 TTY: 1-866-415-8051 Fax: 301-443-4279
E-mail: nimhinfo@nih.gov
Website: https://www.nimh.nih.gov/index.shtml
Organization that provides information for the understanding and treatment of mental illness.

National Sexual Violence Resource Center (NSVRC)

2101 N. Front Street Governor's Plaza North, Building #2, Harrisburg, PA 17110 USA
Phone: 717-909-0710 or 1-877-739-3895 TTY: 717-909-0715
Fax: 717-909-0714
Website: http://www.nsvrc.org/
Advocates and sex offender treatment professionals' network.

National Suicide Prevention Lifeline

Phone: 1-800-273-8255
Website: http://suicidepreventionlifeline.org/

Provides 24/7 free and confidential support for people in distress, prevention and crisis resources for you and your loved ones, and best practices for professionals.

School Nutrition Association

120 Waterfront Street, Suite 300, National Harbor, MD 20745 USA
Phone: 301-686-3100
E-mail: servicecenter@schoolnutrition.org
Website: https://schoolnutrition.org/
Association of school nutrition professionals focused on improving the quality of school meals through education and advocacy.

SHAPE America (Society of Health and Physical Educators)

1900 Association Drive, Reston, VA 20191 USA
Phone: 800-213-7193 Fax: 703-476-9527
Website: http://www.shapeamerica.org/
Organization of professionals involved in physical education, physical activity, dance, school health, and sport.

USDA (United States Department of Agriculture)

1400 Independence Ave., S.W. Washington, DC 20250 USA
Phone: 202-720-2791
Website: http://www.usda.gov/wps/portal/usda/usdahome
U.S. federal executive department responsible for developing and executing federal laws related to farming, forestry, and food.

World Health Organization (WHO)

Website: http://www.who.int/topics/en/
Twitter: https://twitter.com/who
Facebook: https://www.facebook.com/WHO
Organization and resources about projects, initiatives, and activities on health and development topics.

WEBSITES

Alcoholics Anonymous World Services (AA)

P.O. Box 459, Grand Central Station, New York, NY 10163 USA
Phone: 212-870-3400

Website: http://www.aa.org/
Resources and hotline for alcohol drinking problems.

Anorexia Nervosa & Related Eating Disorders (ANRED)

E-mail: info@anred.com
Website: https://www.anred.com/
Comprehensive information about anorexia nervosa, bulimia, binge
   eating disorder, and other feeding disorders.

Anorexia Nervosa Treatment Blog

Website: http://www.anorexia-nervosa-treatment.net/
Blog resource about healthy solutions to eating disorders.

Body Positive

Website: www.bodypositive.com
Tools and resources to feel good about our bodies.

The Body Positive

Website: https://www.thebodypositive.org/
Resources that promote positive body image and size acceptance.

Caring Online

Phone: 1-888-884-4913 or 425-771-5166
Website: www.caringonline.com
Resources for eating disorder treatment. Provides support for speaking
   with a specialist.

Dads and Daughters

Website: http://www.joekelly.org/dads-and-daughters
Resource around father-daughter relationships.

Diabulimia

Phone: 425-985-3635
E-mail: info@diabulimiahelpline.org

Website: http://www.diabulimiahelpline.org/
Resources on education, support, and advocacy for diabetics with eating disorders and for their loved ones.

Eating Disorders Anonymous (EDA)

P.O. Box 55876, Phoenix, AZ 85078-5876 USA
E-mail: info@eatingdisordersanonymous.org
Website: www.eatingdisordersanonymous.org
A fellowship of individuals who share their experience, strength, and hope to help others recover from their eating disorders.

EDReferral.com (Eating Disorder Referral and Information Center)

Website: https://www.edreferral.com/
Provides names of eating disorder professionals across the country by region that can accept referrals.

Food Addicts Anonymous

529 NW Prima Vista Blvd. #301A, Port St. Lucie, FL 34983 USA
Phone: 772-878-9657
Website: http://www.foodaddictsanonymous.org/
Resources for individuals with a food addiction.

Gürze—Salucore

P.O. Box 2238, Carlsbad, CA 92018 USA
E-mail: email@gurze.net
Website: www.edcatalogue.com
Eating Disorder resource catalogue/website specializing in eating disorders since 1980.

Healthy Weight Network

402 South 14th Street, Hettinger, ND 58639 USA
Phone 701-567-2646 Fax: 701-567-2602
Website: http://www.healthyweight.net/index.htm
Resources to research and information on obesity, eating disorders, weight loss, and healthy living at any size.

In Her Image: Producing Womanhood in America

E-mail: InHerImage@juliabarry.com
Website: http://inherimage.juliabarry.com
Information on a multimedia exploration of how popular images represent and shape girls' and women's lives in America.

Intuitive Eating

E-mail: Etribole@gmail.com or elyse@elyseresch.com
Website: www.intuitiveeating.org
Resources about intuitive eating from the authors.

KidsHealth

Website: http://kidshealth.org/
Resources for kids, teens, and parents. Includes resources on various issues including eating disorders.

Love Your Body Project, NOW Foundation

Website: http://now.org/now-foundation/
The NOW Foundation focuses on a broad range of women's rights issues, including women's health and body image and global feminist issues.

Maudsley Parents

Website: http://www.maudsleyparents.org/
An organization of parents who helped their children recover from anorexia and bulimia through the use of family-based treatment.

Media Influence on Body

P.O. Box 191145, San Francisco, CA 94119 USA
Phone: 415-839-6779 Website: www.about-face.org
Tools to understand and resist harmful media messages that affect self-esteem and body image.

Mirror Mirror

Website: http://www.mirror-mirror.org/
Resources and information for people with eating disorders.

Movement Foundation

3045 Franklin Street, Suite 304
San Francisco, CA 94123
E-mail: info@movemeant.org
Website: http://movemeantfoundation.org/#home
Resources and building tools for body-positivity and self-confidence in
   fitness and physical movement.

Narcotics Anonymous World Services (NA)

P.O. Box 9999, Van Nuys, California 91409 USA
Phone: 1-818-773-9999
Fax: 1-818-700-0700
Website: http://www.na.org/
Resources for individuals and families with addictions.

National Association to Advance Fat Acceptance (NAAFA)

Website: https://www.naafaonline.com/dev2/index.html
Resource to empower and eliminate size discrimination.

National Eating Disorder Information Centre

Phone: 1-866-633-4220 or 416-340-4156 (Toronto)
Website: www.nedic.ca
Canadian nonprofit providing resources on eating disorders and weight
   preoccupation.

National School Lunch Program (NSLP)

Food Nutrition Service: USDA (United States Department of
   Agriculture)
3101 Park Center Drive, Alexandria, VA 22302 USA
Phone: 703-305-2062
Website: http://www.fns.usda.gov/nslp/national-school-lunch-program-
   nslp
Resources for a federally assisted meal program.

New Moves

E-mail: newmoves@umn.edu
Website: http://www.newmovesonline.com/

Support to help girls learn healthy eating and physical activity habits while improving self-esteem and body image.

Overeaters Anonymous (OA)

Mailing address: PO Box 44020, Rio Rancho, New Mexico 87174-4020 USA
Street Address: 6075 Zenith Court NE, Rio Rancho, New Mexico 87144-6424 USA
Phone: 505-891-2664
Fax: 505-891-4320
Website: https://www.oa.org/
Worldwide resources for individuals with overeating habits.

Project Heal

Website: http://theprojectheal.org/
Resources and grants for people who cannot afford eating disorder treatment.

Project Look Sharp

E-mail: looksharp@ithaca.edu
Website: http://www.projectlooksharp.org/
Media literacy initiative to provide lessons, media materials, training, and support into classroom.

Promoting Active & Healthy Lifestyles (PE Links 4 U)

Website: http://www.pelinks4u.org/index.htm
Resources for healthy lifestyles.

Pro-Recovery Movement

Phone: 1-888-253-4827
Website: https://www.eatingdisorderhope.com/
Support to help those in eating disorder recovery.

Recover Your Life

RYL Magdalen House 3, Magdalen Street Eye Suffolk IP23 7AJ UK
Website: http://www.recoveryourlife.com/
Self-harm support communities on the Internet.

Screening for Mental Health, Inc.

One Washington Street, Suite 304, Wellesley Hills, MA 02481 USA
Phone: 781-239-0071
Fax: 781-431-7447
E-mail: smhinfo@mentalhealthscreening.org
Website: https://mentalhealthscreening.org/
Screening and mental health programs to reach individuals at all stages
   of their life.

Something Fishy

Phone: 1-866-418-1207
Website: www.something-fishy.org
Resources for awareness and support.

Index

About the Author

Justine J. Reel, PhD, LPC, CMPC, is associate dean for Research and Innovation and exercise science professor at the University of North Carolina Wilmington. Her published works include *Working Out: The Psychology of Sport and Exercise* and *Filling Up: The Psychology of Eating*, both volumes in Greenwood's The Psychology of Everyday Life series. She is also the editor of *Eating Disorders: Understanding Causes, Controversies, and Treatment*. Dr. Reel has recovered from an eating disorder and treated individuals with eating disorders in inpatient, residential, intensive outpatient, and private practice settings.